Seven Keys to a Successful Life

Sue Freeman Culverhouse

Sue Freeman Culverhouse

PublishAmerica
Baltimore

First printing

ISBN: 1-4241-7253-5
PUBLISHED BY PUBLISHAMERICA, LLLP
www.publishamerica.com
Baltimore

Printed in the United States of America

KEYS TO SUCCESS

The two most important questions you will ever ask yourself and, hopefully, find the answers to are:

WHO AM I?   WHY AM I HERE?

I'm sure you're saying to yourself, "She's got to be kidding! I know my name. I know where I live. I already know the answers to those questions."

In addressing the issues of who you really are, you must look deep inside past the facade that the world sees every day.

It's very important that you realize the following:

I am not the color of my hair.
Nor my eyes, nor what I wear.
The skin around me covers me
But I am not whoever you see.

My home may be a tent or cottage small.
Yet where I live does not tell all
Of who I am or why I'm here.

The words you hear me speak today
May n'er reveal what I could say
Of all the depths inside me hidden
Or the truth I know, now written

I am a spirit, soaring free.

5

I came to Earth to learn, to be.

What is my name, it matters not.
The Truth of me is what I sought

My life is but a school for me
To grow, become
To seek
To be.

That's right. Today is the day you can choose to see yourself. Not as your outer being—your physical body, your name, your address, your Social Security Number. Today you can choose to allow yourself to open the way to your inner self, to see what it is in life that YOU really want, to examine your goals, to explore the keys that will help you attain them.

Today is a moment in time that can change all your tomorrows.

I am going to give you a few minutes of time and some space in this book to write down some of your very innermost thoughts. To look at where you are and to see where you would like to go.

Following is a page entitled, "I am." Open your mind and look into your soul. Allow your thoughts to concentrate on you and write whatever comes to mind.

On the next page, you have the opportunity to write "Why I am here...."

I am

Why I am here

LEARN TO KNOW AND LOVE
YOURSELF

How does one get to know oneself?
Day by day, moment to moment, we are changing. We are growing. Every nine months all of our cells are regenerated. We truly are a new person over and over again.

Periodically, we have to stop and take stock of what's going on not only around us, but inside us. All of us have desires that are unfulfilled. Either we have been giving ourselves messages that propel us closer to these desires or we have accepted stumbling blocks that have prevented them.

A simple example is your feet.

How many people reading this page have some type of problem with their feet? I'd venture to guess that a majority do. Either you have a corn or a callous or maybe just a blister on your heel. Because our feet are farther away from our heads than any other part of our anatomy, we tend to leave them until last.

It can be relatively easy to alleviate many of the problems we have with our feet—or even prevent them in the first place.

We can choose shoes that fit well. In my experience, men tend to do a better job at this than women. I think most women choose shoes based on their looks rather than their comfort. High-heel shoes would become obsolete otherwise.

Many times I've run into a shoe store in a hurry, tried on a dozen or so pairs, bought three or four of them after them a maximum of 60 seconds, and lived to take the consequences.

A few simple procedures can alleviate dry skin on your feet. One of the best lotions for feet is castor oil (the type that has no odor, of course). It's inexpensive and it works. (It is also useful on sun-damaged skin to help prevent cancer, I've been told.)

Another simple and inexpensive remedy for feet is a loofah. This simple gourd utilized for a few seconds on your feet once a day can keep calluses to a minimum.

A third wonderful treat for feet is massage. Having your feet rubbed relaxes you all over. One current trend of thought insists that various areas of the foot actually affect various organs of the body. I'm not knowledgeable enough about this theory to comment on its validity; however, I do know that having my feet rubbed makes me feel better all over.

Now what's the point of this little side trip? Simply that something as close to us as our feet can easily become neglected. If that's the case, how much easier is it to push aside that novel we plan to write Some Day or the trip to Europe that we want to take Some Day or that plan to change careers Some Day. We all procrastinate. It's part of the human condition.

Getting out of our easy chair to attend a local concert requires so much more effort than pushing a button on the remote control of the television set. Yet your presence at your daughter's school play—or your absence—may be the source of great pleasure—or pain—to her for the rest of her life.

If you are honest with yourself, you admit that sometimes you'd rather be lazy. Sometimes you'd rather stay in bed than get up. Sometimes you could climb two mountains in one day. Just knowing this helps.

So what are some steps we can take toward loving ourselves?

First, we can accept that we are human with all the joys and agonies that accompany that condition. We all have unique qualities and unique areas of less-than-perfection.

"I'm not perfect" is a very hard statement for some people to make. "I accept myself as I am" is another. Yet both these statements are important because through them, we allow ourselves to know that we are not in a static condition. Just as we could not reasonably expect ourselves to run ten miles when we were six months old, we cannot always expect ourselves to fulfill other people's demands of us, or even all of our demands of ourselves.

One of the tragedies of the present women's rights movements is that we women are laden with guilt if we are not only the perfect career woman, but are the perfect lover, the perfect mother, the perfect everything to everyone. Sometimes we are just plain worn out from juggling a hundred balls in the air at once.

I strongly suspect that we are going to see a generation of women coming along in about 20 years who are going to opt for a little bit of sanity in their schedules. They're going to look back at us and wonder if we'd lost our minds.

So, if you feel tired at the end of the day, it's okay to admit it and prop your feet up for a while.

We are all balancing day by day. What are our desires? What are our duties? What has to be done today? What can I put off until tomorrow? What would happen if I never do that?

When I get in a lather over something of little consequence, I remember one of my father's favorite expressions, "You'll never know the difference a hundred years from now." The next time you have to make a big decision, remind yourself of that and it may put life into better perspective.

Second, you can learn all you can from everyone you can.

That's a very simple but powerful statement. It's okay to accept valid thoughts, translate them into the context in which they work well for you and run with them as long and as fast as you can.

If you see a recipe in a magazine that looks good, you may try it, right? Then what's the difference in seeing someone use a recipe for life that looks like it might be fun or profitable or successful and using it yourself!

Reading biographies is not only an inspiring pastime, it can be extremely profitable as well. If you read the account of the life of Thomas Edison and learn that he found 5,000 ways not to make a light bulb before he ever found one that did work, you can see your own 15 attempts to accomplish your goals as minuscule in comparison. If you read further and learn that he considered these attempts "successful ways to find out what does not work," you can be even more inspired to continue in your efforts.

When I had one of my first jobs after I received my bachelor's degree, I was appalled to be asked to cut and paste parts of scientific papers together so that entire pages of complicated mathematical equations did not have to be retyped. Like most 22-year-olds, I thought I should be given something "more important" to do.

I can't tell you how many times in later years knowing that simple trick bailed me out of a jam.

Nothing we learn is wasted. Somewhere down the road we're going to need it again.

If you look back over your life, you can see certain people who have really made a difference to you. Maybe that person is your parent or grandparent, an aunt or uncle, or a teacher or minister. When you're feeling low—and all of us feel low occasionally—search your memory for the way that person approached a problem. Take inspiration from his/her courage and find your own.

When I was a young adult, I had a discussion with my maternal grandmother one day. She was the wife of a Methodist minister who died in his sleep when he was in his mid-50s. They had nine children, eight of whom lived to be adults.

It was no secret in our family that my grandmother had a favorite child, her second son. He lived in the town where she did and he blew his horn as he drove by her house on his way to work every day. He died of a heart attack when he was in his mid-50s; he was the first of the eight to pass on.

Not long after that, I was talking to my grandmother about her life. She had adjusted beautifully after his death. I asked her what had helped her.

She said, "You know, he was always the one who seemed to need me the most. It wasn't that I loved him more, because I love all my children. So every day I do what it says in the Bible, 'If there be any beauty, if there be any praise, think on these things.' I count my blessings. I have much to be thankful for. It's not that I don't miss him, because I do. But I have children and grandchildren and even great-grandchildren. I have so many people in my life and there are others who have no one."

I have remembered her words so many times and have found the courage to look my small problems in the face and go on.

When I have felt overwhelmed with work, I remember that she reared a very large family in the days before people had washers and dryers.

When I feel poor, I remember that she had many mouths to feed on a country preacher's salary.

No matter who you are or how terrible life seems at the time, there is always someone else who has it worse. You don't have to look far to realize this.

The secret of being happy is to be thankful for all that you have and to focus on your attributes.

Check it out for yourself. Most of the times when we are miserable, it is because we are focused on what we don't have— whether that be material things or good health or whatever—rather than what we have.

Many times we feel miserable in a relationship. We think, "S/he doesn't love me enough. I can't be happy unless I have that love."

We have to love ourselves before we can love anyone else or before we can accept love from another. If we feel unlovable, we either act unlovable or we interpret other's actions as being unloving.

We have to know all the way to the core of our being that we are worthy of love. Each of us is an expression of love in the world. Some days we express that love in more meaningful ways than others, of course.

It is important to look at oneself as a wheel. The rim of the wheel is the outer self that we expose to others—our day-to-day behavior, our personality, our physical appearance. At the center of the wheel is our true self. In that heart of hearts we are perfect beings. If we never look into our center, we cannot express its true light at the rim.

In reality, most of us are clinging to one of the spokes for dear life. We have inklings of who we could be, but we put it off until another day.

I was talking with a friend recently who told me that she has trouble sleeping. She said, "When I start to go to sleep at night, I have all these images racing through my mind."

I asked her if she knows how to meditate. She said she has tried. I replied that there is a simple way to calm yourself when you feel overwhelmed—and here it is:

Get into a comfortable position, either sitting or lying down, and begin to breathe deeply and very slowly. Close your eyes and pretend you are walking down a hotel hallway on the sixth floor. At the end of the hallway is an elevator. You walk into to it and close the door. As you face the door, you continue breathing deeply and slowly while the elevator slowly goes all the way down from the sixth floor to the basement.

When the elevator gently stops at the basement, the door opens slowly and you walk out into a beautiful all-white room with a white movie screen at the end of it. You stand there for as long as you can and watch the white movie screen with nothing on it. If a picture comes into your mind as you look at the movie screen, you gently sweep it away.

When you feel ready, you calmly walk back into the elevator, still breathing deeply and as relaxed as possible. The elevator slowly, slowly goes back up to the fourth floor and you get out.

Then you open your eyes and enter the place where you were before you began this meditation.

It is important to remember that you enter on the sixth floor and get out on the fourth. This symbolically allows you to be in a more relaxed state after your meditation.

If you practice this for 21 days, the time it takes to form any habit, you will become more centered. You will eventually get to the point that you can relax yourself merely by breathing deeply.

This is a simple exercise that anyone can do. It costs nothing but gives great rewards.

You must get to know your inner self in order to become successful in life. How can you express what is truly you if you don't know who you really are!

Third, you can recognize that you have, most likely, up to this point, done the best that you could have with the information you had at the time.

What, you say? What about the time I decided to leave school and get married? I would have been so much smarter to have finished my education first. Yes, that may be true. But, at the time you made that decision, you did not know what would happen two years later. You didn't know what would happen a day later—and you still don't! Do you get the point? We all make decisions based on what we believe or want to believe is the best information we have at the time. Not one person I've ever known is clairvoyant enough to save him/herself grief. Even most people who claim to be psychic don't forestall every pitfall in their own lives, so how can most ordinary people hold themselves accountable for every mistake they've ever made?

No one in her right mind expects a baby to make adult decisions. We try to expect from a child what a child can do. You can't make a three-month-old baby walk—yet we think that we are infallible because we are supposed to be adults.

In truth, each of us is in infancy in some aspects of our lives. Our intelligence and our knowledge do not always equal either maturity of thought or wisdom. Both of these attributes come with experience. No one has experienced everything yet. If you know the stock market is about to crash and you don't try to get out before it does, that's one problem. If you don't know the stock market is about to crash and you lose everything you have, that's another.

Some of us enter relationships wanting to believe that all the wonderful promises of the Cinderella story will come true through the love we want to feel for this person. The other person may be hoping for Rumplestiltskin's wishes, someone who can spin straw into gold. Our dreams are not necessarily those of another person.

Each of us may be looking at the world through different sets of glasses. I may see myself as being loving and giving. The other person may see me as manipulating and grasping. It all depends on one's experience and one's frame of reference, on one's intelligence and one's understanding or lack of it.

We can stand around judging ourselves and others until Doomsday and not necessarily be either right, wrong or even in the ballpark. The inchworm may be measuring the marigolds while a little girl is enjoying its color, an insect is being repelled by it, and a photographer is capturing its beauty. An elephant being examined by three blind people will be described in three entirely different ways. The point is not to waste your life beating yourself internally for the twists and turns in your path. Live through the experience, learn what you can from it, apply it to the next station, and go on with your life.

Some of the unhappiest people on this earth are those who compare themselves constantly to other people. We all know men who feel either terribly superior to their own brothers because the first is a successful physician and has all the money he can ever spend and the other is the owner of a gas station and isn't sure whether or not the new interstate is going to bypass his station. We also know sisters, one of whom is beautiful and secretly envies her sister's success as a businesswoman; on the other hand, the businesswoman is jealous of her sister's beauty and is constantly trying to compensate for her own plainness. How futile!

No orange tree expects to be a dogwood tree, yet we humans can't seem to figure out that our uniqueness is wonderful just the way it is. We can't make ourselves successfully into someone we aren't. That doesn't mean we can learn the skills we need to become a better person no matter what our profession is. It just means we have to accept ourselves, love ourselves, and give life our best shot.

First, we have to know ourselves. In order to do that, we are going to take the time to list several attributes and interests we have as individuals.

First, we are going to write every accomplishment of any consequence we have ever had. This doesn't mean to list "I learned to tie my shoes when I was three" unless you are a person who was born with only one arm. It does mean to list the accomplishments that mean something to you. If pitching a no-hitter in Little League was one of your moments, list it. If giving your favorite doll to a little girl who had no toys was one of your good memories, list it. This is entirely up to you.

This is your list for your eyes only unless you wish to share it with someone.

In the first column, list your accomplishment. In the second, try to focus on why it made you feel happy or that it was important to you or someone else at the time.

ACCOMPLISHMENT	RESULT

Now let's list accomplishments you want to make and why you think it will make you feel good or happy or will be of importance.

GOALS TO ACCOMPLISH	EXPECTED RESULTS

The more you know about yourself, the more easily you can focus on what is truly important to you.

When you know what is important, you can begin to accept yourself.

When you accept yourself as you are, you can begin to set goals for who you want to become.

When you allow yourself to work on these goals, you can ultimately either reach those goals or set them aside and formulate new ones.

When you have reached a goal that is truly meaningful, you will find that you have grown stronger and wiser and more confident that you can reach others.

Always remember: even if you have nothing else in the world or no one you feel that you can trust or depend on, you still have yourself.

Even though at some low ebbs of your life you may think you have nothing, you have much.

Even though you see through a very dark glass at the time, you are never alone. The universe is composed of enough people of good intentions that no one is ever without any support. At any moment in time, you may not be aware of how to reach that support, but that doesn't mean that it is not available.

If you encounter a time in your life where you believe you have a problem that is insurmountable, try this.

Dissect the problem. Break it into as many parts as you can. See if you can solve any tiny part of it. Determine what will happen if you cannot solve it. Ask yourself if a hundred years from now, you will know the difference. Get the situation into a different perspective. Look at it from the top, the bottom, the middle, any other way you can think of.

Ask for help. Work on the problem from every angle you possibly can with your conscious mind.

Then forget it. Go take a hike. Go to a movie. Take a nap. Do anything you can to get away from the problem.

Let your subconscious take over and the solution will eventually come to you. It may not be the solution you imagined. It may not be the solution you want. It may not be what appears to be a positive solution at the time.

Know that this too will pass.

Many times I have been in deep despair; I believed that the heartbreak of the moment was more than I could bear, when the grief of parting was too intense to go on feeling.

But for every lesson I had to learn—and some of them have been horribly bitter—I have come out on the other side more than compensated by the experience. And you will too.

No life is untouched by grief. Whatever we think is important, whoever we believe to be the source of our greatest love will at some time, most likely, no longer be with us.

Grief is felt in direct proportion to the love originally given. When you love someone with all your heart and that person dies or is killed or commits suicide or just leaves you, it hurts.

The pain burns into your soul until you can hardly bear it. You want to deny its reality. You want to pretend that it never happened. You want to run away and hide and never come back to this grief or its source. That's called denial.

Some people enter denial with crutches they carry with them all their lives. These crutches can be bottles filled with alcohol or needles filled with illicit drugs or neuroses from which the person will not turn away. None of them will take away the pain nor effect a healing.

You have to face the pain or lose touch with reality.

You cannot deny grief away. You have to face it and become angry.

You have to feel righteous indignation that this horrible event occurred. It's not fair, you scream. I hate this! I don't want this to be real! I hate everyone who lived when this beautiful soul is gone! I won't let this be! I'm not going to accept it.

Some people get stuck here for the rest of their lives. Many times when people have been married to each other for many, many years, the surviving spouse gets stuck in anger. The anger may cause illness. About 50 percent of surviving spouses get cancer within a year of the death of their beloved husband or wife. The anger may become bitterness. The person may scream out in rage at other family members. The once beloved mother or father may become a tyrant, a seething mass of hatred, a temper-tantrum two-year-old that will not be soothed.

Anger may give way in those who heal to sadness. The tears of grief do not end after the funeral is over or after the divorce papers are granted. They can come at any time—when a favorite song is heard, when the scent of her perfume is perceived on another, when darkness falls and sleep won't come again.

Crying is important in the healing process. It releases in our bodies the chemical outrage that grief produces.

And for grief to end, the grieving must accept.

Acceptance does not mean that the person will ever want to believe that the event occurred, or that all anger has been dismissed, or that part of one's heart will ever be as happy again.

It simply means that one accepts that life must go on. And when one reaches this acceptance, one can begin to live again in a more nearly normal way.

And we all experience grief for the loss of our former selves. Sometimes this comes with a birthday that points out to us that we have not done all that we have wanted to do by this point in our lives. Sometimes it comes when we witness the death of a friend who is our own age, and we have to confront the fact that we are going to die too Some Day. Sometimes it comes when we see gray hair or wrinkles and we know that we are no longer as young as we want to be.

I have always celebrated by saying that I am 21 for the 21st time! And it's true.

That is not to say that our grief for our lost youth is of no consequence; only that it is somewhat a waste of energy.

We all choose what we are doing. We can choose to spend four hours weeping and wailing and gnashing our teeth because we don't look like a movie star or we can spend the same four hours working out on a treadmill, taking a hike, writing a letter to a friend, eating something healthful, or whatever other positive experiences we can encounter.

When we feel sad, we can say to ourselves, "I'm sad because I miss him very much. I loved him deeply and he loved me. He is gone from my life now and I shall always miss him, but he would want me to be happy and productive. I am going to cry until I can feel able to stop crying. Then I am going to wash my face, comb my hair and call a friend who may be feeling as lonely as I am right now. I cannot express my love for him but I can give what I have to someone in need."

We can choose to go onward and upward, no matter what blow we have been dealt.

In 1980, I wrote a history of a tuberculosis hospital. I interviewed a lovely woman who had had many difficulties in life but was always a blithe spirit. She began by saying, "I simply adored TB! When Mother would say it was time to do the dishes, I could feel very unwell. I got out of more things that way."

We don't hear much about duty in the 1990s, but it was once considered in polite society that one's duty was to be cheerful. When you think about it, cheerfulness makes life more pleasant for everyone—the person who is cheerful and those around him.

In the biography of Beverly Sills that I read once long ago, I remember Ms. Sills' mother saying about her that she was not a happy woman (both Beverly Sills' children were born with disabilities), but she was a cheerful woman.

It is much more healthful to smile than to frown—and a smile makes many fewer wrinkles!

Here's a list of a few other ways, simple ways, you can start being good to yourself.

1. Give yourself something special every day, even if it's just an ice cream cone, or a long bubble bath, or an hour to read a book you've been wanting to read. Remind yourself that when you do that you are worthy of good things.

2. When you wake up in the morning, think of something you have to look forward to that day. If you can't think of anything, plan something right then.

3. Learn that bad weather doesn't translate into "bad day." The weather is something over which we have no control. Our attitudes do not have to sink because it rains.

4. Simplify your life as much as possible. Stop joining groups because you think you should. If your goals do not mesh with those of an organization, put your energies elsewhere. Try to create as many positive experiences for yourself as possible and you will attract further positive experiences. If you're bored standing around at parties where you talk to people you have no desire to know, choose an alternate activity. If you meet someone in whose company you enjoy being, cultivate that friendship no matter what the social status of the person. Cut through the behavior you think you should enjoy and choose the behavior that you do enjoy.

5. If you were a child in your family who was expected to be nearly perfect, learn that making nearly perfect endeavors is okay no matter what the social status of the person. If you find yourself berating yourself with your inner voice screaming names like "Stupid" or "Bimbo" or worse, remind yourself—even aloud—that you are intelligent and capable—and that the world will keep on turning even if you made a slight error. Dropping a book or having to retype a document won't make any difference in the grand scheme of life. Everyone makes mistakes and so do you. Accept that premise and do the best that you can: forgive yourself if it isn't perfect.

6. Cheer yourself on as the day passes. Whatever goes right in your day is cause for celebration. Remind yourself: I found a good

parking place; I got my reports done on time; I had a healthful lunch; I called a friend who needed encouragement…. Make yourself a beautiful day.

7. Don't push yourself beyond your limitations through lack of paying attention or diffused focus. If you are a person who needs a while to wake up, get up early enough before you have to meet someone else's schedule so that you have time to drink your morning coffee and have a shower and dress without hurrying. If you oversleep, don't panic and race helter skelter. Recognize that it is better to miss half an hour's pay than to have an automobile accident. Give yourself a break.

8. If you find yourself getting sick often, think about the parts of your body being affected. Is something breaking your back, or making you want to scream to the point that your throat is sore? Is there something in your life you need to get up and out so that your respiratory system has "caught cold" and is expelling? Have you made yourself so anxious about an upcoming event that your digestive tract is reacting adversely, or are you withholding from someone or something so tightly that your digestive tract can't act? Or are you avoiding an event by becoming sick? I know a person who becomes ill every time she is scheduled to go out with a certain "friend." She actually dreads seeing this person so much that she becomes ill to avoid the meeting. Your body will tell you a great deal about the stresses you need to address. Listen to it and your health will improve.

9. Have a place for everything and put it back after you use it. The outward sign of a creative mind is a chaos of flotsam and jetsam. Create more room for creativity by sorting out the clutter on a regular basis. Let your environment reflect you. If you need more peace in your life, create rooms that are neatly organized and use restful pastel colors in them. If you thrive on excitement, choose vibrant colors and unusual shapes. Even better, have certain areas of your home for each type of experience, some with a busy feel and others for rest.

10. If you have a choice of what to do, do the thing you hate to do first and get it out of the way. If you put off doing the thing you dread, your foreboding will cloud the fun experiences. This is the first step to self-discipline.

11. If you find a luxurious item that you have always wanted and you can buy it for yourself—either outright or on a layaway plan—and you know you are going to regret it for the rest of your life if you don't, then go ahead and buy it. Even though some acts appear frivolous to others, it is okay to pamper yourself. You are worth it. It is important to place value on yourself and love yourself so that others can learn to do so as well.

12. Expect good things to happen to you. If you are going to shop in a crowded area, expect to find a parking place near the door. If you are going to a dinner party, expect to meet someone who is interesting. If you are entering a drawing, expect to win. By creating a feeling of positive events about to happen in your life, you will project a positive feeling around you. You will begin to receive what you are sowing.

13. Learn to experience silence. Everywhere we go, we hear background music, traffic noises, television, noises of all kinds. Choose silence as often as you are able to do so. This is time for you to become calm, to reflect on ideas, to search for questions and answers you need to know.

14. Practice active listening to others. Accept the wisdom that they may be relating to you. If you never truly pay attention when someone else speaks, you may miss something important. I read once that most people who commit suicide have said so, often repeatedly, and no one paid attention. Listen to the words other people choose and you will glean information about their state of mind. It is tragic that most relationships, those between lovers, those between parents and children, those between friends, end up being on a superficial level only because we simply do not listen carefully to what is being communicated by the other person. If you cultivate friendships with other people who have acquired the art of listening, you will benefit as well.

15. Watch as many sunrises and sunsets as possible. Let the beauty that unfolds become part of your soul.

16. Look at the stars and project your perspective from their view looking down on the earth. Know that if you have to be separated from the one you love, the distance between you is minuscule when seen from a star.

17. Learn to be kind to yourself and others. Demands are resisted. Requests are special roads. "Please" and "thank you" are still the magic words.

18. Read as many books that expand your mind as you can. Choose self-help books, biographies of successful people and people who overcame adversity, travel journals, trade publications. Keep current on your field of interest. Check out videos and tapes from the library. Borrow from friends who have books that they have found helpful. Always expand your mind as much as possible.

19. Take at least one new seminar or class every three to four months.

20. Share yourself with others. Make time for children and seniors. Tell your loved ones that you love them, even if you don't always like their behavior. (Remember: they probably don't like yours all the time either.) Volunteer where you are needed. Be a real friend, not just when good times come, but when tough ones roll around too.

21. Behave in ways you like and applaud yourself for right choices. Be the best role model you know how to be. You never know who is watching you and is trying to emulate your behavior.

SET MEANINGFUL GOALS AND ALLOW YOURSELF TO REACH THEM

Each of us justifiably has goals we want to reach in life. We may not have sat down to write them out, but they have been in our minds for a good portion of our lives, whether we have recognized them or not.

First of all, we have short-term goals. They include such things as eating each day, washing our hair, brushing our teeth, buying supplies we need for the week, making sure the car is filled with gas, having enough money to pay our bills, getting to work on time, etc.

Then we have medium-range goals. They might include acquiring a new vacuum cleaner or taking a seminar before summer comes or establishing a savings account.

Then there are long-range goals. Here come the hard ones: buying a house, purchasing a new car, taking a dreamed-of vacation.

All of these goals are important. But like everything else, they need to be organized. And here's your chance. We are going to write down at least five goals in each category. You can write down many more than five if you want, but five can get you started. We'll use two columns, one for the goal and the other for its approximate cost. Remember to include not only items to buy but job changes you may want to make or personal improvements like education. Don't write just the goals you think are easily reached. Write down the ones you've always dreamed of. If you've truly desired to go to Europe, write it down even if you can't imagine ever having enough money to go.

Long-Range Goals

GOALS	APPROXIMATE COST

Medium-Range Goals

GOALS	APPROXIMATE COST

Short-Term Goals

GOAL	APPROXIMATE COST

Now we have something with which to work. Next you need to list all the sources of money you have: salary from your job, stock premiums, savings interest, raises annually, bonuses, incentives, alimony, child support, rebates from coupons, gifts, etc. Wherever you receive money is a potential for meeting your goals.

Let's take saving for a vacation as an example. You say, "I never have enough money left over for a vacation." Let's see if there's some way we can find to change that attitude.

First, do you think you deserve a vacation, or is there some reason you of all people on this earth must work 24 hours a day, seven days a week while others while away their hours? Okay. You deserve a vacation too.

Where would you like to go? Do you want to spend one night in luxury or a week in the sun? Do you want to go from here to the next town or would you like to take a trip around the world?

Okay, you've decided where you want to go, how long you want to stay, and about how much money you need for the trip.

At this point in time, you have enough money to meet your monthly expenses but there's never anything left over. You have some choices. How can you make extra money? You could save aluminum cans and recycle them. You could go through all your belongings and sell the ones you don't need. You could cut coupons from the newspaper and magazines and save all the money you save from them. You could get a temporary part-time job (baby-sitting, delivering newspapers, working on Saturdays for a few months in a retail store) and save the money. You could save all the money you get from your birthday and Christmas and any other occasions.

There are many ways to save money (many more will be discussed in the next chapter) for the vacation you want.

One way that some people meet long-term goals is to refine your budget and have two savings accounts. It works like this. First, make a commitment to yourself to save one tenth of every dollar that passes through your hands. In other words, pay yourself first.

"But I can hardly make it now," you say. Just try it for a month. If you never see the money, you can't spend it. When your paycheck arrives, put one tenth in savings. Pay the bills, even if it means making a smaller payment than you usually make. Just keep putting one tenth away so that you can't spend it.

If you have any money at all left each month after all your bills are paid, put that immediately into a separate account. All the money books tell you to keep at least three months' salary in savings for emergencies, but few people can do that.

However, if you begin to save for something special and really work at it, you will be surprised at how fast the money accumulates.

Another important factor is to discipline yourself not to tap this money at the first sign of a change in your money situation. If you have forgotten about a bill and it must be paid, by all means, dip into your savings and avert disaster (like having your electricity turned off), but don't consider deciding that you're depressed and need to go on a drinking binge an emergency!

Let's take a goal that doesn't require money. Let's assume that you want to have more free time. Look at your schedule. Do you spend time on some activities that you strongly dislike? Perhaps you can find a way to trade duties with someone else in your household so that you avoid spending part of your time this way. Do you want more time to read? Make sure you have a book beside your bed, in the bathroom, beside your chair in the television room.

Of course, we are now assuming that you have made the decision that you are worthy of having more free time. Your basic attitude is the first step in reaching any goal.

Now let's look at freeing yourself from the kinds of feelings that sabotage your reaching your goals.

Consider your childhood. In your family were you the first child, the middle child, the youngest, one of the pack? Were you always the one who was supposed to behave responsibly even though another child could act in frivolous ways? Did you think that your parents wanted you to be a girl (if you are male) or to be a boy (if you are female)? How did this affect the way you look at yourself, even now?

Were you supposed to be a clown and make people laugh? Did you grow up trying to entertain your mother because your father was always at work and didn't have much time for either of you? Did you have to go to work at an early age so that you missed a great many ordinary childhood activities?

Where did you fit in your family drama?

How are you still relating to the world because of these early childhood events?

Many people actually sabotage their lives by almost reaching the point where they become wealthier than their parents or have greater public notice than a brother or sister. Suddenly a deep sense of guilt overcomes their desire to reach success and they literally sabotage themselves. Sometimes artists set out on an expansion of their work—a series of paintings or a grouping of pieces of sculpture only to be overwhelmed by an inability to finish even one piece. Their fear of success is so great, they become paralyzed.

The same thing can happen to a writer. The expectation that a critic may dislike the book may override the joy of writing it to the point that the writer gets writer's block and cannot put a word on paper.

Think about the event of your life. Try to see yourself in the family drama, keeping in mind that each of us still has a small child within that needs nurturing. If that child's fears are uncontrollable, we can fail.

Sometimes people set out a path of failure in order to wound a parent or other loved one. Some children, before they acquire enough maturity to realize that no parent is perfect and no childhood is perfect, sabotage their own lives in order to humiliate the parent. Some teenage pregnancies occur for this reason. Some young people engage in crime and continue to do so over and over so that they are certain they will be caught for this reason. Through inflicting pain on the "cruel" parent, the person sabotages his/her own life—and perhaps the life of an innocent baby as well.

Each person must examine his own heart and mind constantly to understand what behavior she/he is exhibiting and why.

One woman refused to have children to the point that her husband, who wanted a child very much, left her. It never occurred to her that she did not want a child because her own brother was killed in an accident. The pain she felt and the pain she witnessed in her parents was so intense, it convinced her that she would never have a child of her own. But she never confronted this reality until she had reached the point in her life when it was no longer possible to have a child.

It is difficult to see ourselves as others see us. We have to get reflections of ourselves from those who love us enough to be truthful with us.

We can reach almost any goal we set for ourselves, but we must be honest, brutally honest, with ourselves. We have to make sure our goals are truly what we want. We have to examine not only our present feelings but our past experience as well.

Success is defined by each person. If your belief that success can only come to you when you have a million dollars in the bank overrides everything else in your life and you believe you can acquire a million dollars, you can do this. If you define success as having a mate who truly loves you and you persist in becoming a loving person, you will attract someone into your life who can fulfill this role.

Whatever habits you have that you want to change can be initiated by writing this down, reading it over for 21 days, and working towards the change for that period of time.

If you have always believed you were doomed to be poor, you can change your mind and change your life.

If you have always believed that success was for someone else, you can reprogram your mind to know that you too can be successful.

Try this exercise. Write down in the next few minutes three goals that you want.

Now write down all the objections you can think of that could prevent your having these three things.

Now write down your game plan for how you can overcome these barriers and get what you want.

Go to seminars not once but several times a year. The intellectual stimulation is wonderful, not only from an educational standpoint but from a sense of personal fulfillment as well.

If your goal is to find a new job, use the following resources to your best advantage:

1. Ask family and friends to keep their ears open for you. More new jobs come about by word of mouth than any other way.

2. Study the want ads seriously on a daily basis. Learn what firms have to replace workers frequently. This indicates either that it is either a very large business with many jobs or that the firm has low pay scales so there is a constant turnover or that someone in the structure is difficult to get along with and can't keep help. Use your own judgment; if this is the type of atmosphere in which you think you will be happy, go for it. My advice is to look elsewhere.

3. If you are locked into your present location, your game plan might, at first glance, seem to keep your efforts directed at local jobs:

however, with current computer technology, you may be able to work for a firm that is located elsewhere and fax your information to the home office. This is particularly true in sales. A friend of mine recently found a job selling convention space for a hotel at the other end of the state from where she lives. She sends her correspondence over e-mail to a secretary located at the home office; it is typed and then sent back to her. She works completely from her own home—tax deduction for a home office and all!

4. Make sure you have a professional resume to present no matter where you apply. Tailor the resume to fit the job and write in your cover letter that references can be supplied on request. This allows you to select appropriate references for each particular company to which you apply.

5. Wear the most professional-looking clothing you own when you are interviewed. A good rule of thumb is "the more skin you show, the less professional you look." No see-through blouses, no micro-mini skirts, no low necklines, no floor-length skirts, no hats allowed! Women should wear a basic suit or dress with dark shoes and matching stockings (no patterns please!) and minimal jewelry. Men should wear a dark two- or three-piece suit and coordinated shirt and tie, dark socks and lace-up shoes. The more serious you look, the more serious the interviewer will feel that you are in approaching the job. Let the interviewer set the tone for the interview. Don't offer a "hail fellow, well met, back-slapping" attitude. Be friendly, polite, and businesslike.

6. Before you accept a position with any company, make sure you know what your working hours will be, what benefits are offered (insurance, sick leave, vacation, retirement, incentives, etc.) Find out how long it will be before you are eligible for sick leave and vacation. Make certain the company is following federal laws concerning overtime.

7. If you accept a job only to be offered a much better one right away, don't hesitate to move on if that's what you want to do. No decision except death is set in stone.

MAXIMIZE USE OF YOUR TIME AND RESOURCES FOR YOUR HIGHEST GOOD

Agreed, everyone has the same 24 hours in a day.

But, you say, not everyone has the same demands on those 24 hours.

How right you are!

For every person there are almost infinite ways to use one's time. Just look at a few of them. Here's a sample of what most people do some or part of in a week:

1. Eat
2. Sleep
3. Engage in sexual activity
4. Work/go to school/earn money
5. Buy food
6. Pay bills/manage money/go to the bank
7. Wash clothes/take clothes to the dry cleaners
8. Shop for weekly needs, special occasions
9. Entertainment/recreation/television/sports/reading
10. Personal maintenance: physician/dentist/chiropractor
11. Family responsibilities: care of others
12. Spiritual growth: church/volunteer work/prayer
13. Setting goals/planning for the future
14. Resting/relaxing

Now you can see why you're tired sometimes.

Truly, time management is one of the real challenges of life. Each of us has to be on guard not to let one of these areas get out of balance, either by too much or too little. For instance, sometimes we get so busy with work that we have very little time for our family or for cleaning the house, whatever else may slide by the wayside.

So what are some guidelines we can use to see that we don't get our agendas out of kilter?

I enjoy reading about Albert Schweitzer, a Nobel laureate, Bach scholar and concert organist; he was a physician and genuine humanitarian. He raised money to go to Africa and build a clinic in the middle of the jungle. Without going into all his capabilities, I shall share with you what I learned about his life that has helped me tremendously.

Albert Schweitzer was able to work 20 hours each day. The way he did it was by switching from one type of task to another every few hours. For instance, he would work very hard physically for four hours, then he would stop and move on to practicing the organ for several hours. At that point, he would switch to seeing patients and later he would write. By going from one type of activity and level of concentration to another, he could sustain a much longer work day. He lived to be more than 80 years old and accomplished more in one lifetime than most people accomplish in three or four.

What I learned from him, I put into practice.

In 1988, I started a business. It was the joy of my life up to that point, but for various reasons, it failed.

I found myself divorced, $35,000 in debt, and looking for an entirely new career.

I found a job taking care of a 92-year-old woman who had been so difficult to get along with that it was either hire someone at that point in time or she would have to enter a nursing home.

My work schedule began on Sunday night after which I stayed in her home until Thursday morning when a nurse came to relieve me. This nurse and another took two-day shifts until my return on Sunday night. I was in charge of obtaining all food for the household, seeing to her personal needs, cooking during my shift, seeing that her medications were properly administered, and dealing with her behavior.

On my days off, I worked several other part-time jobs. Each of these jobs entailed other types of work that were totally different from what I did for her.

When it became necessary for this person to enter a nursing home, I began to take care of a man in his eighties who was recovering from cancer. I worked with him 18 hours a day, seven days a week for eight months until he began to recover to the point that he needed me only 12 hours a day. His wife was able to care for him during the day by herself. Until then, he had awakened me about every 15 to 20 minutes all through the night.

When I look back on those months, I sometimes wonder how I survived.

One way I coped was by pampering myself every way I could at the time. (Remember: I was paying back $35,000 in addition to my ordinary living expenses.)

I listened to wonderful classical music every day.

I had my hair cared for professionally every week.

I dressed up in my best clothes every day.

I talked about my frustrations to my friends.

I paid on my bills as much as possible without depriving myself.

I gave myself rewards at various times throughout the three years it took me to clear the $35,000 from my list of bills.

I learned that I could set a very difficult goal and reach it if I gave it my best.

Whenever I wanted to give up (I could have gone bankrupt and started over), I looked around me and counted my blessings.

For instance, during the years I was working like this, the United States was in a recession. Many heads of corporations were losing their jobs. Many people could find no work.

I reminded myself constantly that I was making more money than many presidents of corporations. I reminded myself that I had a job when others didn't. I reminded myself that my working conditions were far superior to those of many other people; after all, I was in air conditioning in the summer and had plentiful heat in the winter.

Always remember: you are stronger than you know.

LEARN TO MANAGE MONEY SO THAT IT WORKS FOR YOU

"Everything comes to he who hustles while he waits," Thomas A. Edison once said.

We're all waiting—waiting for our next promotion, waiting for our tax return, waiting for retirement, waiting for our ship to come in. All things come to those who wait.

The question is, "How are we spending the time we have while we're waiting?"

I once knew a woman who wrote a book while she was waiting for her son to practice baseball. Every day during the summer, she took a notebook with her and wrote while she was waiting for him. During one summer season she completed her first book.

If you write only one page a day, at the end of only one year, you will have written a 365-page book. Large projects taken in small increments become much more manageable.

Keep a notebook with you at all times so that you can jot down whatever thoughts you have that you need to remember. If you're working on getting your budget in order, keep a record for one month of every single penny you spend. At the end of that time, place in categories each expenditure so that you see where your money is going.

IN ORDER TO PLAN A BETTER PATH, IT IS IMPORTANT TO LEARN WHERE YOU HAVE BEEN AND WHAT PATTERNS YOU HAVE FORMED AS YOU TRAVEL.

What does money provide for you?

Beyond necessities, beyond security, beyond entertainment, money widens the scope of your choices.

41

One of the basic tenets of success is your perception of what success means to you. What success means to someone else may be completely different—or even totally at odds—with what success means to you.

Success happens at many levels of existence. Here's some food for thought:

PHYSICAL REALITY

A. Food

Does success mean to you that you can stock your kitchen with six months' worth of every food imaginable?

Does it mean that you can afford to have a cook?

Does it mean that you can eat every meal in a restaurant, or that you can eat out any time you want to?

Does it mean you can afford to fly to Paris for dinner if you have a whim to do so?

Or does it mean you have enough resources to establish your own soup kitchen to feed the poor?

Or would you rather be successful at growing all your own food so that you know what you're eating and what's been sprayed on it, or that nothing has been?

Do you prefer to eat alone, in the company of another, or in a large group?

I heard some friends tell of a multi-millionaire who asked his wife to ask one of the servants to bring him a fried egg sandwich. She replied, "Dear, don't you remember? This is a holiday. We have no staff today." He said, "What good does it do to have all this money and I can't even get a fried egg sandwich when I want one?"

Obviously, having skills other than acquiring money is rather important.

B. Clothing

Do you want six closets full of designer fashions and a thousand pairs of beautiful shoes?

Do you want to have a full-time servant who takes care of your clothing and dresses you every day?

Do you desire to have jewels and furs at your disposal?

Do you want a wardrobe consultant who chooses everything for you?

Are you interested in being able to go into any store in any city in the world and buy any piece of clothing you want?

Are you contented to simplify your wardrobe to the point that you have only a few choices but each selection is something you genuinely enjoy wearing?

Do you want all new articles of clothing or would you prefer to buy nearly new items at one tenth the price?

Do you want to live in so comfortable an environment and climate that you have to wear only a bathing suit or actually go nude a good portion of the time?

Do you even care what you put on in the morning or do you see your clothing as an extension of your personality?

C. Shelter

Do you want to live in the mountains, in a valley, in a desert, by the seashore?

Do you like sunshine, snow, tropical breezes, changeable climate, rain daily?

Do you want to hear English spoken all day or would you prefer to be one of only a few English-speaking persons in town?

Does your house also need to encompass your work place?

Do you need garage(s) for your vehicle(s), barns or stables for your animals, landing pads for you airplane or helicopter?

Do you want to live in a one-room contemporary, a Georgian mansion, a camper?

Do you need separate rooms, movable walls, 20 bedrooms, 12 baths? Do you want room for many guests or would you rather no one came to stay overnight?

Do you want music available in every room, a television in every seating area, a greenhouse or atrium, a Jacuzzi in every bathroom? Would you like a waterfall on your property or a spring that vies you a private water system?

Do you require your own generator or are you secure with the local power company's offerings?

Do you want extensive gardens filled with trees and flowers or a tiny plot mowed by the homeowners' association?

Do you want a staff of 20 or do you prefer to take care of all your own needs?

Do you wish for servants' quarters as part of your residence or do you want full privacy?

D. Lifestyle

Is being the CEO of a corporation your dream? Does that include the long hours at work, the reduced family life, the travel, the "keeping up with the Jones"?

Do you want more time to be at home so that work and home blend together? Do you have the self-discipline it takes to leave the television set behind and close the door to your home office so that you can accomplish a day's work?

Do you want to be a jet-setter who lives out of a suitcase? Do you feel comfortable at very formal dinners or in the thick of a heavy discussion of the financial markets?

Does the simple lifestyle at a cloistered monastery appeal to you? Can you deal with deprivation and isolation?

Do you want a life of service to others? Can you sustain your own health when you have very few financial resources and are constantly exposed to the diseases that many times accompany poverty?

Are you willing to sell your choices to a corporation where decisions regarding where you live, when you will move, etc., are many times out of your hands? Or can you work for the government or armed services where these decisions are made on needs of others rather than your personal goals? Is a commune for you? Can you see yourself bartering for many of your necessities rather than utilizing a traditional monetary system?

PERSONAL FAMILY NEEDS

A. Personal Preference

Do you like to sleep late or rise early or stay up all night and sleep during daylight?

Do you need eight hours of sleep a night, or can you survive better on four?

Do you need a quiet home where you can retreat from the world, or do you like a household full of children and animals?

Do you tolerate older people/young children/teenagers in your everyday life? Do you feel happier with people of other ages or do you prefer being with people your own age?

Does your sleep become interrupted by the slightest sound or can you sleep through sirens? Do country night sounds lull you to sleep or terrify you?

Are you horrified if someone enters the bathroom while you are brushing your teeth, or are you happy in a Jacuzzi full of naked people?

Do you require city lights and nightclubs in your immediate vicinity, or is the seclusion of a mountain cabin closer to your heart?

Does your home need to be filled with light, or does the darkness give you a sense of security?

Do you want your picture on every television new show or do you prefer to be anonymous?

B. Family Requirements

Do you want a mate?

Do you want a formal marriage or alternative lifestyle?

Do you want to have children, either your own or adopted ones?

Do you have elderly parents for whom you are responsible?

Do you want to live in a singles-only area or do you prefer a family neighborhood?

Do you like to visit relatives daily/weekly/monthly/yearly/never?

Are you the parent of a school-age child?

Are you able to make financial decisions based on your own personal needs or must they consider family obligations as well?

Do you have loving relationships in your life or are they filled with arguments and strife?

Have you been divorced or are you contemplating divorce? If so, is your situation amicable or a major source of grief?

Is your extended family comfortable with your present lifestyle or is this a source of contention?

Does your health or that of a family member require scheduling around medical appointments on a frequent basis?

C. Spiritual Requirements

Are you extremely involved in spiritual study or church activity, or is this a plane of life of little or no importance to you?

In your interactions with others, do you ask yourself first, "What's in it for me?" or are you more concerned with the welfare of the other person?

Do you feel business is business no matter what the consequences, or are you first cognizant of your belief that whatever you dish out, you'll have to eat later?

Do you need other people around you who share and reinforce your spiritual beliefs, or do you need a quiet place for meditation alone?

Do you have a religious center to which you feel the need to live nearby?

Does the idea that being successful can only come to you if you are willing to walk over other people and their feelings ring true to you? Do you believe that wealthy people all got their money by cheating other people out of it?

Do you think that life is over at death or that life is only a prelude to an afterlife?

Do you believe that only poor people are acceptable to be candidates for sainthood?

Do you think that good people are not concerned with money?

Do you feel that humility is more important than accomplishment?

Do you see your sphere of influence as being only in your immediate area, or do you see yourself as able to influence people throughout the world?

Do you have a hero? A role model on which you would like to base your life? Someone whose mistakes you plan to avoid?

What does the concept of God mean to you? Is God a non-entity, a scary man on a throne in the sky, an inner spirit who guides your life, a stranger, a mystery to you?

Do you believe that God punishes people for their wrong-doing? Do you see God as the ultimate source of love? Do you think that you are out of the realm of God's notice?

Have you ever contemplated the concept of God? Do you believe that God has been created in man's image and that each man, therefore, sees God as he wants to?

How does your idea of God's presence or lack of it translate into the way you treat other people? Into how you spend your money? Into what goals you have for your life?

D. Age Requirements

If you are younger than 30, how do you see yourself at age 55? 65? 85?

If you are 40 or older, do you see yourself as wanting to retire from your career, or do you want to work every day of your life for as long as you are physically and mentally able?

47

Does your physical environment need to reflect any physical handicap needs you may have? Do you need ramps in your home so that if either now or at some future time someone requires use of a wheelchair there is accommodation for it? Do you see the time when pull bars in bathrooms will be needed equipment in your home?

Do you see advancing age as something that happens only to other people, or do you acknowledge that you may confront the repercussions of old age yourself?

Do you have a family history of people who live to be 100 or more? If so, have these people maintained good health in their later years? Are there health conditions in your family that tend to reduce one's life expectancy?

Do you require fitness equipment in your home, or do you want to live in a neighborhood where it is safe to go for long walks, or do you want to live near a spa or fitness center?

E. Career Requirements

Do you want to work?

Do you want to travel in your work?

Do you need to be in an office or do you prefer a classroom or van in order to accomplish your daily tasks?

Do you want to be the boss or have someone else direct your activities?

Do you work well alone, in a small group, on an assembly line, with a computer as an interface?

Do you want to dress up when you go to work, or do you prefer to wear more leisure-type clothing?

Do you want to work in a room with other people or do you need a private place with no disturbance?

Do you want to live in/near/or a long distance from your work environment? Would you like a career that you can conduct no matter where you are? Does working from a hotel room appeal to you, or do you need your own home available to you at the end of the day?

Is your title important to you? Do you want to be the head, considered part of management, or part of the clerical or support staff of your enterprise?

Are you more interested in working for a service industry, a wholesale/retail type enterprise, health care, public service, entertainment, or other type of enterprise? Do you want to be a member of the class of people who have only social activities as their focus of concern?

Do you want to deal with the public on a daily basis?

Are you interested in investing and living only on invested money? Are you knowledgeable in this area, or do you have someone you can trust to take care of your money?

Do you feel comfortable taking risks with your money, or do you absolutely require knowing what your income will be monthly to the penny?

Do you have expectations of inheriting money or do you believe your only income ever will be derived from your own efforts?

Do you want to get up in the morning knowing you have a planned agenda or would you rather be free to do whatever strikes your fancy?

Do you want someone else to handle your money or do you want to deal with all aspects of it yourself?

Do you require the security of all types of insurance, or do you think your money is better invested elsewhere?

Do you truly believe your only hope of becoming wealthy is contingent on your winning either the lottery or Publishers Clearing House Sweepstakes?

Do you have a hobby that appeals to you more than your present career? Could you convert that to being your vocation? Would you be happier working at your hobby than at your present career?

Do you require monthly income in regular equal payments or can you handle the stress of feast-or-famine occupations?

At what point in yearly income would you feel that you have become successful? $25,000 a year? $50,000 a year? $100,000 a year? $250,000 a year? $1 million a year? The interest from $2 million a year?

Do you need stair-step plateaus to feel you are reaching success or do you think one fell swoop is the answer?

Do you feel that need to communicate your knowledge to other people or does holding your wisdom as a personal secret make you feel more powerful?

If you required the direction of other people's agendas as part of your success, are you interested in enhancing their lives, or would you prefer the flinging of more hurdles into their paths?

Would you rather be in any other possible situation rather than having to discipline or fire an employee?

Do you have enough self-discipline to regulate your own activities so that you can reach your goals?

Do you have enough self-confidence to admit you are wrong and to change directions?

Have you ever moved to a new location because you felt the success of your career depended on it?

If you had to choose between relocating because of work and making your loved ones very unhappy—even if it were a temporary condition—or staying where you are and feeling that you are stagnating, which would you choose?

These are by no means the only questions one must ask oneself when considering success. They are beginning guidelines to assist you in getting to your basic feelings about money/success and what is preventing your having what you want.

THOUGHTS HELD IN MIND PRODUCE AFTER THEIR KIND.

If you believe in your heart of hearts that you are never going to be anything but poor and that you do not deserve to be wealthy, you may at some time in your life acquire a great deal of money, but you may at that point sabotage yourself so that you lose it.

Let's look at some ways people sabotage themselves with money.

Most of us are taught from an early age that certain types of behavior—whether from a religious, moral or social standpoint—are less desirable then others.

Let's take smoking as our first example.

In the early decades of this century up until the time that the link between smoking and disease was publicized, smoking was portrayed in movies, through advertising and socially as being a glamorous activity engaged in by macho men, femme fatales, and the sophisticated elite. It was presented as being sexy, sensuous and socially correct.

Now smokers are in social and medical disgrace. If you are hooked on smoking, you are relegated to back alleys and out of the public eye. Smoking is literally being legislated out of public places.

Aside from all the other reasons that smoking is considered undesirable, let's look at its day-to-day cost (not taking into account possible medical costs that might arise from it).

Let's assume that a pack of cigarettes costs $2.00. Here's what that translates into (if the price remains the same over a long period of time):

	One Pack	Two Packs
One day:	$2.00	$4.00
One week:	$14.00	$28.00
One month (30 days):	$60.00	$120.00
One year:	$730.00	$1,460.00
Five years:	$3,650.00	$7,300.00
Ten years:	$7,300.00	$14,600.00
Twenty years:	$14,600.00	$29,200.00
Forty years:	$29,200.00	$58,400.00

Now let's suppose you drink a six-pack of beer a day for the same lengths of time (assuming again that the price does not go up):

One day:	$4.00
One week:	$28.00
One month:	$120.00
One year:	$1,460.00
Five years:	$7,300.00
Ten years:	$14,600.00
Twenty years:	$29,200.00
Forty years:	$58,400.00

If you drink two packs of beer a day, or a bottle of cheap liquor, or drink a pack of beer and smoke one pack of cigarettes a day, you are going to spend about $116,800 in a period of forty years if the price doesn't go up—and have you ever seen the price of these items go down dramatically? No.

For a person who thinks he can afford a $20-a-day pot habit, he will spend the following:

One day:	$20.00
One week:	$140.00
One month:	$600.00
One year:	$7,300.00
Five years:	$36,500.00
Ten years:	$73,000.00
Twenty years:	$146,000.00
Forty years:	$292,000.00

Or, even beyond belief, a $100-a-day cocaine or heroin habit:

One day:	$100.00
One week:	$700.00
One month:	$3,000.00
One year:	$36,500.00
Five years:	$182,500.00
Ten years:	$365,000.00
Twenty years:	$730,000.00
Forty years:	$1,460,000.00

This is why people end up stealing or being dope pushers themselves. And these simple charts do not take into consideration the misery brought into the life of the person who is the addict as well as that of the people who love them.

Nor does it take into consideration the loss of work because of health problems, the waste of resources considering what else this money could have been used for, and the loss of time the person could have spent in other pursuits.

Also, many of these 20- and 40-year figures are meaningless because the person doesn't live that long. I would venture a guess that every person who ever reads this book has within his/her acquaintance (and/or family) one person who has led a tragic life because of one of these addictions.

How many people have actually lost their freedom and have been incarcerated because of one of the addictions? Or has met death by accident or suicide directly because of this type of behavior? How many innocent people have been victims of disease or death because of these addictions?

Aside from these bank or stock investments, what are some other avenues that you can consider?

Life insurance is considered by many people to be a scary proposition. Many people totally refuse to become involved in life insurance because it makes them confront the idea that some day they will die. It is human nature to resist death and even the subjects that involve death.

Many people believe that if they buy life insurance, they will attract the attention of the Grim Reaper and He will come calling. The truth is that the only people in our society who can afford to be without life insurance are those who are independently wealthy. A funeral is an expensive proposition. Loved ones are extremely vulnerable emotionally when someone dies. If there are no provisions for death expenses to be taken care of, it can create tremendous hardships. Most funeral homes will put immediate liens on possessions if cash is not provided, either from one's bank account or from insurance.

Your own particular needs will determine what type of life insurance you buy.

Term insurance is provided by many companies in the amount of one year's salary for the person. This is, most of the time, enough to cover funeral expenses and very little money left over for the survivors. Social Security will provide a very small payment, usually about the amount required to open and close a grave.

Term insurance pays only on death. It is the cheapest form of life insurance available. Many bankers will advise you to purchase only this type of insurance.

Insurance companies have whole life and universal life policies available as well. These types of policies pay the person monthly payments when the policies mature.

Insurance is a specialized branch of investment. Knowing the integrity of your insurance agent and checking what you have been led to believe with your banker is sound business.

Investing in real estate is another avenue for acquiring wealth and/or major headaches.

One of the wealthiest women in the 1980s had only a fifth-grade education. Her husband and she had invested heavily in real estate. She owned 47 pieces of property—some single-family dwellings, others that were duplexes, and still others that were multi-unit apartment complexes. She was by any monetary standards a successful woman.

However, she had made some rather unusual decisions. She did little or nothing to keep up her property, choosing only to collect rent. Instead of adding to the value of her holdings, she left her children a gigantic mess.

Second, during her lifetime, she did everything she could to pit her daughter and son against each other. Neither one could enjoy the wealth she left them because they battled over the estate and its disposition for years. One wanted to sell and divide the money; the other wanted to hold on. The attorneys gathered the spoils of the battle.

Third, while the woman lived, she dressed as if she were practically penniless. She never bought any new clothing, choosing to wear her son's old house shoes and dresses she had made herself that were beginning to wear out. When she had to enter a nursing home, the nurses—believing her to be on welfare—were about to take up a collection to buy her some better clothing—until they learned the truth about her financial condition.

Fourth, she ended her life in loneliness. Most people who came to see her did so out of duty rather than affection.

Success, like beauty, is somewhat in the eye of the beholder.

Measuring one's worth by the amount of money in one's checking account may be a poor measuring stick. If you look around you to see who leaves this life having lived each day to the fullest, you may be surprised to see what success requires. It is not only money but a cheerful spirit that proves successful when ultimate worth is counted.

This does not mean to imply in any manner that acquiring wealth by owning real estate is a poor choice. On the contrary, the path to wealth by owning real estate may be more easily accessible to a great many people than various others.

As in any financial venture, one must first arm oneself with as much knowledge as possible.

Read, talk to professionals, immerse yourself in examining as much real estate as possible. After all, what other business is as open for scrutiny. Every week there are hundreds of houses on the market where Realtors are happy to let you look, ask questions and find ways to buy. Devote your extra time to looking; it will pay off as you learn more and learn to ask better questions.

Align yourself with trustworthy people. Check out the reputation of Realtors, accountants and attorneys in the area who claim to be knowledgeable. You will find a variety of degrees not only of knowledge but integrity and foresightedness.

Be open to creative financing.

The first piece of property I ever owned by myself came to me purely by "accident" or fate, however you wish to look at it.

I was talking to an acquaintance, a person I knew to be honest and trustworthy, after a meeting one day. He mentioned that he had a piece of rental property he was about to put on the market. I told him I was looking for an investment in real estate. As we discussed our plans, I learned that the house was in exactly the price range I could afford and that for me, he would be willing to finance it himself at half a percentage point higher than the bank was offering at the time. Since we both used the same lawyer for our business, we decided that we could trust him to handle the transaction.

I saw the house, loved it and bought it with no Realtors' fees, no bank charges, and only minimal attorney's fees. I was able to rent it out very shortly after that. The house has proved to be a good home for my reliable tenant, a good investment for me and a good source of monthly income for my friend. He helped me decide what expenses the property would cost me each month so that I was able to have all of them included in the rent I charge. I financed the house for 15 years and its value is increasing with each.

The house in which I lived at one time is an example of creative financing. I had a lease purchase agreement. A large portion of the rent I paid was applicable to the down payment. The owners, who were transferred to the West Coast, had the knowledge that I took excellent care of the property and was adding to its value. I had the joy of living in a beautiful location with the option of remodeling the house to suit my taste. The improvements I made to the house were part of the lowered rent I was able to negotiate.

It is my personal experience that living in a house before one buys it is essential.

I once had a lease purchase agreement on a house that appeared to be an excellent buy. After I moved in, I discovered a score of major problems that were evident only as one lived in the house. I ended the contract with a loss of $3,000 that would have gone to my down payment had I bought the house, but I saved myself at least $30,000 I would have had to invest in the property had I bought it. The grief I saved myself in having to deal with major construction faults not of my making would have been immeasurable.

Never be too small to admit that you have made a judgment that needs correcting.

MAKING A MISTAKE IS PART OF THE HUMAN CONDITION. ADMIT IT. CORRECT THE ERROR INSOFAR AS POSSIBLE; LEARN AS MUCH AS YOU CAN FROM THE EXPERIENCE. RELEASE IT WITHOUT GUILT AND GET ON WITH YOUR LIFE.

I know of a man who spent his life acquiring property which he rented and then financed for other people to buy, if the situation arose. When he died, his son sold everything and invested the money in tax-free bonds so that he could live off the interest.

The son's reasoning is that he did not like being a landlord. He could not handle being awakened in the middle of the night to be told someone's furnace was out of order. He did not like to deal with tenants who did not pay rent on time. He wanted to devote his life to other pursuits. He made the right choice for him.

Don't be afraid to choose your own path. People who enter a profession to satisfy other people's expectations of them are seldom happy or nearly as productive as they could have been had they chosen the path because of their own inner needs.

Not everyone can deal with similar types of stress. Being a landlord is a source of pleasure to some people; to others, it is a nightmare.

Be honest with yourself and do what works for you.

Buying and selling is another type of money-making enterprise. I once interviewed a landscape architect who designs the exquisite flower beds at Walt Disney World. When I asked him what the most important thing to remember was, he replied, "Don't forget to put the tall stuff in the back and the short stuff in the front!"

The most obvious has to come first.

In buying and selling, the cardinal rule is "Buy low; sell high." If you don't make a profit, you're out of business. Another basic bylaw is "Never run out of cash." If you have no money, your business ceases to exist.

Simple ideas like selling many items with pennies of profit have revolutionized retail. People have been finding this type of "building a better mousetrap" since bartering began for the cave man.

You can too—if you put your mind to it.

Here are some things you should remember if selling is your forte:

1. Offer a better product at a better price and you'll beat the competition.

2. Give better service and what the customer wants and people will beat a path to your door.

3. The greater the turnover, the greater the profit.

4. Don't get complacent: the early bird still gets the worm. While you're resting on your laurels, the competition isn't.

5. The customer—within the bounds of reason—is always right. You're not doing him a favor; he's supporting your life and its needs. Acting as if he's an intrusion is financial suicide.

6. Rules were made to be bent if the customer's needs require it.

7. Some difficult customers who consistently and obnoxiously make your life a misery are people you can exist without. If you have

to jeopardize service to other customers because this type of person is being so difficult, you can cheerfully ask them to shop elsewhere. 8. Saving time for your customers keeps them coming back. Customers have many choices, including shopping at home. Don't force them to wait to be served or, even worse, to pay you. The next time they may go to your competition. 9. Location, location, location. Just as in choosing real estate, the location of your business can either nearly guarantee you success or failure. You can have the most wonderful product offering on earth, but if your customers can't find you or a place to park, you have lost your shirt.

AGAIN, ALWAYS REMEMBER: NO PROFIT, NO BUSINESS.

Before you go into business, make sure you have enough money (aside from what you invest in the business) to support yourself for two years. This is not optional. Most small businesses fail because the owners do not utilize this information.

Colleges now have seminars for new business owners or entrepreneurs who want to go into business. Take advantage to these classes, many of which are free.

The Chamber of Commerce has an affiliated group called SCORE. These retired business executives offer free advice for anyone wishing to enter business. You can make an appointment, take your business plan with you, and get the advice of someone who has been there and knows. Listen and heed it.

We have discussed very briefly many ways to make money. What about how you handle it after it is yours?

Benjamin Franklin described a happy man as one who has a penny left after his expenses are paid and a miserable one as one who lacks the last penny to pay them.

123 WAYS TO SAVE MONEY

1. Never buy deposit slips from your bank; ask the teller for free ones.
2. Try never to write a check for less than $25.00; if a bill is less than this amount, write it for two months. (For instance, if your cable bill is consistently $15.00 per month, pay one month in advance.)
3. Put any unexpected income directly into your savings account; since it is unexpected money, you won't miss it from your monthly budget. You'll be surprised at how fast it can add up.
4. Always get at least three prices on any major purchase before you buy. It is possible to save more than $100 on an appliance and even $1,000 on an automobile, van or truck if you look around.
5. Take someone you trust with you when you shop for clothing. Get the other person's opinion before you purchase. What may look good in the mirror may not look good in three dimensions. Money wasted on something you leave in the closet is money you could use elsewhere or save.
6. Learn price codes in department stores so that you know if an item was brought in as a sale item or if it was part of the original merchandise for the season.
7. Buy linens during January when prices are cheapest. Linens are also on sale in August at most department stores.
8. Make certain you get a receipt for donated items so that you can use them as a tax deduction. Ask your accountant to keep you advised on the latest tax rulings concerning charitable contributions.
9. If you are having great difficulty making a decision, don't buy anything. Chances are something better is going to come along.
10. Don't drive into an unsafe area to buy gas a few cents cheaper. Getting robbed is a very expensive way to try save money.
11. Buy in bulk whenever possible if you have storage space. Not only will you save time in having to shop more often, you'll save on travel for the extra shopping trips.
12. Stay out of stores. The more often you shop, the more tempted you are to buy.

13. Never buy items next to the checkout; they are usually well inflated and are put there to tempt you.

14. Ask for discounts whenever you pay cash, especially if you are dealing directly with the store owner. Any credit card purchase costs the store, so it can give you several dollars off and still come out ahead of where it would be had you charged an item. (That does not include the department store's own credit card because the store makes high interest if you don't pay your bill each month.)

15. Should you have any error in your billing, make certain the incorrect amount of interest you have been charged is also removed from your account.

16. When you are hired into a new job, negotiate as many extra benefits as you can: free parking, pretax deductions for health insurance, pretax medical expense deductions throughout the year, employee discounted-in-kind services (meals in restaurants, discounted tires in tire store, etc.), free dental/visual insurance, bonuses based in yearly or quarterly results, etc.

17. Open a business of your own that will include travel expenses, office supplies, etc., so that you will be able to shelter some of your primary income tax time. Work with your tax accountant to see what works best for you.

18. Establish good credit as soon as you can, so that if you need to buy a vehicle or home, you will have good references.

19. If you have credit cards on which you are paying high interest, pay them off with a lower interest Visa or Master card, if possible, or with a lower interest bank loan if that is available.

20. Pay off any high-interest loan first, then the next highest, etc.

21. Avoid charging anything you can. If you must charge, ask yourself first if you are still going to want this item as much in another year when you are still paying for it.

22. Shop around for no-interest buying. Many stores are offering major purchases for no interest for three months, six months, a year or even 18 months to entice customers to buy.

23. Always ask questions before you sign any contract. Make sure you understand the terms, or else consult an attorney before you sign.

For instance, if a store offers "90 days interest free" does that mean you have to pay in three equal installments or can you pay the entire amount on the 89th day and still pay no interest?

24. Make sure there is no penalty for prepayment on any loan. A loan that has "simple interest" means you pay interest only on the amount left; other loans may charge interest on the entire amount until the entire loan is paid off. Still other loans make you pay almost all the interest first and then you begin to pay on the principal.

25. Never borrow money from a "finance company." These firms charge as much as two to three times what you will pay at a bank or even on a credit card.

26. If you can negotiate a private loan at a slightly higher rate of interest than banks are charging (from a reputable person whom you know to be honest) and can get a signed legal contract on the amount you are paying, do so. You can save hundreds of dollars on "lending fees" and hidden costs the bank may charge you.

27. It is possible to deposit money in a certificate of deposit with a bank, borrow that same amount of money to use for some other purpose, then pay off the loan at the end of that time; use the interest you have earned to help pay off the loan. You will save money in the long run because the interest you earned will offset the loan. If the loan involves real estate, it may also be tax deductible. If you have made payments during the life of the loan, you may actually be able to keep your original amount of money that secured the loan.

28. Establish a savings account at your bank even if you have very little money in it initially. When you apply for credit, the fact that you have a savings account will be helpful.

29. Get a regular savings plan established, even if it is only a few dollars a month. Ideally, you should write yourself a check directly into your savings account for ten percent of every paycheck you earn. If it is gone at the beginning, you will get used to living on the income that is left. If you think you will wait and dump whatever is left over into the account, you may not have anything left to dump.

30. Never close out your savings account even if you have to take out everything except the minimum amount. Start over and eventually

you will come out ahead. Make sure the bank is not going to charge you a fee that will take your entire minimum amount, however.

31. Save all your change at the end of each day. Deposit it once a month on your savings account so that it can earn interest.

32. Never, never build up a huge checking account unless you have an interest-bearing checking account. The bank is using your money every day it is on deposit; make sure you are getting your share.

33. If you have at least two months of income on deposit in a savings account that is easily accessible, you can then begin to utilize other forms of saving. Certificates of deposit for long terms (one, two and five years) pay higher interest usually than a regular savings account.

34. Savings and loan banks ordinarily pay higher interest than commercial banks; be sure your account is federally insured, however, if you choose this method of savings.

35. Individual retirement accounts are excellent ways to save for retirement and shelter part of your annual income. New rulings allow for early withdrawals in case of family medical emergency, the purchase of a first home (not rental property), college tuition for a child, and other circumstances. Discuss all the ramifications of this type of saving with your tax accountant so that you can maximize your utilization of this type of saving.

36. Mutual funds, stocks, bonds and other types of investment carry risk. A recent study by a major television network pitted a monkey, a 12-year-old child and a stockbroker against each other in choosing stocks. At last count, the monkey was ahead.

37. If you must play the lottery, limit yourself to the amount of money per week you are willing to donate as an equal amount to charity. For instance, if you play $2 on Wednesday and $2 on Saturday, give $4 a week to the Salvation Army or some other charity. Then add an addition $4 a week to your savings account. If you win anything playing the lottery, add it to your savings as well. (Remember: all unexpected income goes towards savings.)

38. Inventory your wardrobe every three months. Anything you have not worn for the past year either must go to a charity or be sold in a consignment shop. Exceptions can be evening wear, special sports equipment (ski clothing, etc.), and inherited clothing (your grandmother's wedding gown).

39. Sort through your household goods every six months. Any items you no longer need or use should be sold in a yard sale, through a buy-and-sell newspaper, or in a consignment shop. Make sure you keep current on collectible items that may be worth more than you originally paid for them so that you don't sell a now valuable item for a tenth its worth.

40. Don't hesitate to buy recycled goods. Nearly new clothing (some of it may still have the original sales tags) can be purchased through second-hand stores.

41. Watch for double-up sales on clothing—"all already marked-down items on sale at an additional 30%!"

42. Don't hesitate to use store coupons. It's considered chic, not cheap. And watch for stores that give double the value on coupons. You can save a sizable amount on your groceries.

43. Keep a running list of items you need so that each time you go to the store, you keep current. Try never to go to the store for only one item.

44. Keep your medicine cabinet well stocked with common cold remedies, medicine for upset stomach, aspirin-type medications, burn creams, and other common ailments. Buy these items on sale before you need them rather than having to pay full price when an emergency arises.

45. Locate stores that sell food items cheaper because they buy in bulk and package themselves. You can save as much as half the cost of the item this way.

46. Keep some homemade toys on hand for children. Boxes with wooden spoons, a strainer, small metal pans, wooden blocks, and other household items will fascinate a child longer than expensive store-purchased toys.

47. Create gifts for your friends and family members by using your own talents. A calendar made with your own pictures as

illustrations, a recipe book full of family favorites, an address book compiled on your home computer and bound with a unique cover, your own homemade jams and jellies can make a birthday or other occasion extra special.

48. Grow as much of your own food as you can. If you don't have room for a garden, grow tomatoes, peppers, onions, herbs in pots.

49. Make out menus for all meals weekly before you go to the grocery. Buy all the ingredients you need on the weekly shopping trip. If something comes up that you have to change your schedule or eat out unexpectedly, you'll be that much ahead for the next week. Be sure you plan one meal each week with creative use of leftovers— soups, a vegetable pie, turkey hash; make certain this meal is something to look forward to, not something to dread.

50. Always make up ground beef into patties and freeze it so that you can choose the amount you need for the meal you are preparing. If you freeze ground beef in a large lump, you may need only a third or half of it for one meal and will then have to cook the rest very soon or have it ruin.

51. Keep plenty of freezer bags, plastic wrap, aluminum foil, and other food-saving items on hand. Wasting food is very expensive and counterproductive. Buy all sizes of plastic containers with lids and use these before considering expensive packaging listed above.

52. Choose nutritious foods first and buy as few junk foods as possible. For instance, potato chips are not only high in cholesterol and fat, they cost as much per unit as very expensive beef considering what you are getting.

53. Buy only the amount of fresh fruit you can eat before it ruins. This is one type of item that spoils quickly and needs careful planning.

54. Plan at least one meal a week utilizing dried beans. They are excellent in reducing cholesterol, are very inexpensive and are very versatile.

55. Keep plenty of chewable toys for your pets. They are less expensive to replace than a piece of furniture or door should your pet become bored.

56. Rather than decorating your home with prints, buy paintings from an unknown artist whose work you consider excellent. If the person becomes famous, your painting may be worth many times its original value.

57. If you need furniture upholstered, take it to a school where upholstery is taught. Many times you can get the labor free.

58. Barter for everything you can. By trading something you don't need or want for something you do, both you and the other person can come out ahead.

59. Share your talents and knowledge with young people. They will learn as they help you accomplish tasks you may not be able to perform alone.

60. If you have extra storage space in your home, consider renting it. Many people have items they may need to store temporarily.

61. The public library is one of the greatest sources of wealth you will ever find. You can ask for any book to be ordered that is not available. You can get free information on any subject. If the local library doesn't have it, the staff can acquire it from another library. You can get movies, tapes, compact discs, books on tape, foreign learning courses, and hundreds of other items through a library. You can even borrow pictures for your walls.

62. If you have sufficient cash saved for an emergency, you should choose high deductible amounts on your car and home insurance. If you have little or no savings, you are better off to choose low deductible amounts.

63. If you have a hard time saving, buy a life insurance policy that forces you to save and will pay dividends after you are retired. If you are a disciplined saver, choose term life insurance that will pay only at your death. A life insurance agent will point out that term insurance is good only if you die and should you have to terminate your coverage, you get no money back. A banker will tell you that you should buy only term insurance because he would rather you invest the money you would pay for other life insurance with the bank.

64. If you are buying jewelry as an investment, be aware that it is very hard to recover the original price of any stores when you resell

them. If you are buying jewelry for sentimental reasons or because you enjoy wearing it or giving it to someone else, enjoy it for its beauty and leave it to your heirs.

65. A jewelry store in Nashville, Tennessee, used to have its sales slogan, "If you don't know diamonds, know your jeweler." Consider that many discount houses are selling you inferior stones that are flawed; that's how they can sell them at a "reduced price." If you don't know the difference, it may not matter. If you are concerned with buying a high-quality stone, buy from a reputable jewelry store that has been in business for many years and has a good reputation.

66. When you travel and want to buy a "souvenir," buy local art. You will not only take home some of the culture of the area, you may help perpetuate an ancient means of expression that could be lost otherwise.

67. When you are seeking entertainment, support local theater, music, art, and dance. Not only are these events affordable, they are the wealth of any community. Don't consider these events as part of the audience only. Become involved. If you have no wish to perform, volunteer to help with sets, costumes, lighting, publicity or other important supporting roles.

68. Buy early tapes of compact discs of local artists. If they become famous, you have invested wisely. If they do not, you may have discovered talent no one else will ever hear.

69. Always buy the best toilet paper you can afford. If you can have only one luxury, at least don't feel like you have to settle for the "gas station" variety.

70. If you want to own an expensive car, visit showrooms and learn as much as you can about them. Even if you have to wait years to buy the car you want, you will at least be armed with knowledge when the time comes. If you want to own a mansion or expensive yacht or whatever, go where these items are and learn all you can. Imagine yourself as being successful enough to own whatever it is that you want. The more you dream, the closer you come to positioning yourself to the fulfillment of your dream.

71. Save but don't hoard. Understand that the money you are saving is to accomplish your goals. Just having the pieces of paper

themselves should not be the focus of your attention. Too many people begin to become afraid to use the money once it is theirs. Money is a commodity of exchange. In itself, it is only a dirty piece of paper.

72. Check all charges on every bill; make certain you know not only what you are being charged for but why. For instance, you may be charged for using a trash receptacle owned by the trash collectors; you might be able to buy your own for the cost of renting it for two months.

73. Consider vacationing by house-sitting for someone in a desirable location. If you live near the mountains, you might be able to swap with someone who lives at the beach.

74. Vacation costs can be cut considerably if you work with a professional travel agent. Many package deals include transportation, airfare and meals at a bargain rate. Make sure your travel agent has actually been to the location that is your destination so that you are receiving firsthand advice.

75. Save yourself as much as the cost of a trip by reading carefully before you book. If you want to see local culture and sample exotic food in a foreign location, don't travel to areas that cater traditionally to tourists; you might end up with many souvenir shops, Americanized food and imported entertainment.

76. Consider choosing a study vacation that may be tax deductible. Many universities or private consulting firms offer courses in resort areas that combine business and pleasure.

77. Don't buy travel packages as a "contest winner" through the mail or over the phone. Many of these "winnings" are condo promotions that require your listening to sales pitches on your trip and varying degrees of pressure to buy. If you want a bargain, get to know your travel agent or learn from friends who have visited the area.

78. When you are on vacation, take enough money and plan to spend enough money so that you can enjoy your trip. One person and her husband spent every vacation staying at the YMCA and eating frugal meals so that they could attend her husband's favorite theater productions. Although she wanted very much to go to Paris, she

acquiesced to his wishes to go to London each year. After he died, she went to Paris alone with the sad realization that her dream was incomplete without him.

79. If you want to save on meals during your vacation, eat fruit and cereal in your room at breakfast, have a sumptuous meal at lunch when prices are more reasonable, and a light dinner. Or if you go to an expensive restaurant for dinner, order an appetizer, salad and dessert.

80. While you are on vacation in a foreign location, get to know native residents and find out where they eat and shop. Not only will you save money, you will see more of native culture.

81. Unless you have studied rules of the road extensively, do not drive in a foreign country. The complications if you are involved in a traffic accident can more than override any savings you thought you were making. Or, if you should make a mistake and encounter the local gendarmes, your encounter with the law might prove not only costly but might end your vacation on a very unhappy note. Have your travel agent arrange transportation for you if possible. Otherwise, the hotel concierge can help you.

82. Respect the religious customs of the area you visit. You should find out ahead of time if you will need to have your head covered in a cathedral or if you're wearing red may signal to locals that you are a prostitute.

83. If you have binoculars, cameras or other equipment with you in a foreign country, don't fall for the "Let me look through your lens" trick only to watch your equipment disappear into the crowd.

84. No matter where you are traveling, find out what areas are most likely "dens of thieves" and avoid them. Many areas are safe during the daytime but are suicide after dark. Be aware and KEEP OUT.

85. If you are accosted by a robber, give him your material goods and keep your life, if possible. Playing hero looks fine on television but is not a healthful leisure activity. Almost any material good you own can be replaced, but your life can't. If you find yourself in trouble with others nearby, yell "FIRE!" to attract attention. You are more likely to obtain assistance than if you yell "HELP!"

86. Keep a list of all your credit cards, their numbers, and the emergency 800 number for each in a place other than your wallet. If you are robbed, notify the police first and then notify your credit card companies so that you will not be charged for any amounts the robber may place on your account.

87. Buy your rings to fit so well that it is very difficult to take them off. Most rings are lost because people take them off to wash their hands or the dishes. Either the person walks away and leaves the ring on the sink only to have it stolen, or the ring is knocked into the sink and never recovered.

88. Never invest in jewelry thinking it will be easy to recover the original amount. A "precious stone" is precious when the jeweler sells it to you. When you try to sell it back, you will be fortunate if you can get 25 percent of your original investment.

89. Jewelry that is so expensive that it must be kept in a safety deposit box is too expensive to own. Wear your jewelry and enjoy it; insure it and relax.

90. If you want your jewelry insured, be certain that your homeowner's policy covers it. Often expensive jewelry requires its own rider. Check with your agent to be sure it is also covered.

91. Preventive maintenance on almost anything you own is much less expensive that major repairs due to neglect. Burning out a motor because you forgot to add oil is an expensive lesson. Read manuals of appliances and machinery you own; keep up regular maintenance and you'll come out ahead.

92. If you buy a computer, make sure initial instructions are included in the price. If you agree to buy the computer and the salesperson offers to install it for $75 an hour, tell him you've changed your mind and will buy it elsewhere. You may be amazed at how quickly the price of installation goes down; if it doesn't, walk out the door.

93. Try to buy any major appliance or piece of furniture where the store delivers it free. Injuring your back while you haul it yourself is not a way to save money.

94. If you can safely perform household repairs, do it yourself. If not, leave it to the professionals. A young surgeon decided to save money by painting his house. He fell from a ladder and was paralyzed as a result for the rest of his life.

95. Keep backup sources available for emergency power outages if you live in a cold climate. If you have to purchase a kerosene heater when everyone else in town is out of power and needs one too, you may find it either unavailable or more expensive than during warmer times.

96. Arrange for snow removal before it snows. Services contracted for before they are required are not only less expensive; they are then available to you first. The same is true of items like salt and chemicals to melt snow and ice. As in other emergencies, be prepared.

97. When you invite dinner guests, serve inexpensive meals you can prepare in advance. In winter, a nourishing soup or pasta dish followed by a fruit and yogurt dessert can fill the bill. In summer, a special salad followed by a seasonal fruit pie can be spectacular. Don't feel that you have to torpedo your budget in order to entertain.

98. If you give a party, serve punch rather than mixed drinks. Be sure to cut off any service of alcohol at least an hour before your guests leave. In some states, a party giver can be held liable if a guest becomes inebriated and is later involved in an accident. Have people spend the night rather than drive with alcohol in their systems.

99. Give your parties at the same time of year each year. Each year add a new item for service. For instance, if you have a Southern theme, buy oversized soup cups and saucers to hold chili one year; the next year add a colorful tablecloth; the third, buy cactus drink glasses. Your friends can join in the fun by adding a pennant as a holiday gift. Your collection can be the theme for a much anticipated yearly event.

100. Set a dollar limit for gift giving. Decide before you go to stores what you plan to give each person. Give in to impulse buying only if you find an item on sale that will fit the person and occasion better. Since you know what birthdays are coming up in the following months, plan in advance and watch for items to go on sale rather than waiting until the last minute and paying top dollar.

101. Choose a theme for gift giving at Christmas or Hanukkah. One year give warm clothing. Another give something red for each person. Still another, give a piece of sports equipment. This centralizes your shopping area rather than requiring you to drive all over town.

102. Economize on wrapping paper, bows, etc., whenever possible so that you can spend more on the gift than the wrappings. Buy after Christmas when prices are as low as a fourth of the original. Buy inexpensive tissue paper and add stickers. Or use Sunday comics. Hoard shopping bags year round to transport gifts or use instead of wrappings.

103. Coordinate your wardrobe so that you can wear three or four pairs of shoes (all black or brown) with every outfit. Women should wear opaque stockings in winter; they not only last longer than sheer hosiery, they are warmer. Men should buy seven pairs of one color of socks so that they never have a sock with no mate.

104. In general, try to buy the best quality of everything that you can possibly afford. In the long run, the better quality item will last longer and tend not to have to be replaced when it is least convenient.

105. Women should shop for evening wear throughout the year whenever it goes on sale. Since an after-five gown is worn rarely, it should not be the most expensive item in one's wardrobe. The best choice for any wardrobe is a basic black dress than can be combined with various jewelry, jackets or other accessories to make several interesting outfits. Another good choice is a fancy white blouse and plain black skirt. Any brightly colored or boldly figured combination is easily remembered and will require replacement sooner.

106. Men can build a wardrobe around a basic suit in black, brown or navy, a sport coat that coordinates with the suit, two pairs of coordinating trousers, and several matching shirts. Ties are an important part of any male's wardrobe and should be carefully coordinated with the basics. The classic navy pinstripe suit and a navy blazer are great additions to any man's wardrobe. A plaid suit is a loser.

107. Check with your bank for free booklets on how to save money. Get to know your banker and ask for help. If this money expert doesn't have time for you, change banks!

108. Subscribe to cable television if you are a television watcher. Use educational channels as much as possible to increase your knowledge. Check into courses from local colleges that give credit for televised classes. You not only save time in travel to and from college, but wear and tear (and gas) on your car.

109. If you like to go to movies for entertainment, consider subscribing to one movie channel from your cable service. The $10 or so it may cost you for the movie channel is minuscule compared to the price of a theater movie, popcorn and drink.

110. Take advantage of free or half-price specials for specialty channels on your television cable service. Note on your business calendar the date the special ends and have the service removed. These specials are run frequently so you can take advantage of one frequently.

111. If you watch television infrequently, take only basic cable service or don't have cable at all. It is cost effective only if you utilize it more than half the days in a month.

112. Keep good records throughout the year so that you can utilize every tax deduction. Remember to include all business gifts and other business expenses. Recent tax laws have allowed large deductions annually for small businesses for purchase of equipment. Keep in close touch with your accountant for new changes in tax laws so that you can take advantage of whatever deductions apply to your situation.

113. Use a tax service unless you use the easy 1040 or the short form for your taxes. Tax laws change so frequently that it takes an expert to keep up with them. The cost of a tax service is also tax deductible. One person I met had lost out on claiming the interest on her mortgage for 15 years because she did her own taxes. This one deduction—one of the major benefits of buying one's own home— was lost because she thought she was saving money by calculating her own taxes.

114. Shop for new insurance coverage at least once every two years. Rates vary dramatically from one company to another. Many times you can get lower rates if the company writes both your car and homeowner's or renter's insurance. Ask for nonsmoker's and accident-free driving discounts also.

115. Weigh options of towing service against the cost of one towing, or the inconvenience of having to pay cash for towing if you are caught on the road. Check AAA fees versus insurance rates to decide which option to choose.

116. Let the person in your family with the best financial mind handle the finances. If one partner can't keep the checkbook balanced or is a compulsive spender, give this person an allowance and let the other partner handle the money.

117. Make sure you plan the budget as a family. If children understand that there is a pie with various pieces and only so much to go around, they are less likely to be ever demanding. Budgeting teaches good habits early in life.

118. Allow children to have their own bank account as soon as they are old enough to understand the concept of saving money. Portions of all monetary gifts should be deposited by the child after a mutual decision is made. If the child is allowed to spend 50% of a gift and s/he sees her/his savings grow as well, s/he may decide to deposit more of the money him/herself.

119. Many accountants advise having home businesses hire children so that income can be distributed in more accounts for tax purposes. Children should acquire a Social Security number by the time they open a savings account; this is required by law.

120. Get to know a good financial advisor. These people have many vehicles for the growth of money. Small savings can grow to very handsome sums of money if saved regularly over a long period of time. Get good advice and follow it.

121. Don't hesitate to use two savings accounts for different sets of goals. You should have one savings account for immediate emergencies and another for long-term goals with the objective of never touching the latter until the goal is reached.

122. Learn to stop before you buy. Ask yourself, "Is this something I need or something I want or just a whim?" Especially before making a large purchase, think it over for a minimum of one week.

123. Get to know salespeople. If you have a salesperson from whom you buy frequently, the person will begin to let you know when special sales events are coming up. S/he will steer you toward quality products that will last and away from items that will not serve you in the long run.

NOW THAT YOU HAVE A BEGINNING, START YOUR OWN LIST OF MONEY-SAVING IDEAS. KEEP YOUR BOOK WITH YOU AT ALL TIMES SO THAT YOU CAN COMPARE PRICES.

GOOD LUCK!

DEVELOP RELATIONSHIPS THAT SUPPORT YOUR BEST SELF

Each of us is born with two fears: the fear of falling and the fear of loud noises. All other fears are learned.

How do we learn these fears?

We are taught them in the fabulous school of life.

Our parents are our first sources of fear acquisition. It is these wonderful people who teach us to fear getting burned, who teach us to look both ways before we cross the street so that we don't get run over, who teach us to fear going up to animals with which we are unfamiliar so that we have less chance of being harmed by their teeth or claws or fangs.

Our parents (or step-parents of foster parents or whoever our initial caretakers happen to be) also teach us that some of our fears are groundless.

Many small children at some stage of development believe that they can be sucked down the drain of the bathtub like the water is. It takes some more experienced person to point out that we are larger than the hole in the drain and, therefore, can't go down the hole.

When we are small and young, we have very little control over who is teaching us. If we are fortunate we have loving caretakers who have minimal fears—and who give us the straight story on what is a positive fear and what is a negative or foolish one.

However, no one grows up with a complete set of accurate facts.

In actuality, we all have to learn and/or relearn many things, even as adults.

I grew up with some pretty fantastic ideas—one of the worst of which was about human nature. Somehow it escaped me that there are people in this world who enjoy being cruel/dishonest/mean/ hateful to others. It took me some time to get this idea straight.

Because I had falsely assumed that if I exhibited these qualities in my relationships with others, I would receive the same treatment. Wrong.

So I had to readjust my expectations of what I could expect from others not once but many times.

This lack of "fear" of the dark side of human nature was as important to my reaching success as the releasing of an inordinate fear of success is for some other people.

A woman once reminded me, "All men are liars. It says so in the Bible."

So now we are at the crux of choosing positive relationships. Where does our sensible side that expects good results from a relationship draw the line with our cautious side that knows some of the negative results from people who, even though they may have good intentions, may actually harm us?

It's true that no one speaks the truth one hundred percent of the time. We all tell someone they look fine when the person may be having "a bad hair day" because we feel we are being kind by telling "a little white lie." On the other hand, if we become involved with a pathological liar, we are in for some serious problems. The problem with a pathological liar is that the person believes what he's saying to the extent that you tend to believe him even though there's a nagging feeling you aren't being given the straight scoop.

And if you happen to have fallen in love with the false image the pathological liar has projected, you don't want to be confused with the truth until it absolutely smacks you in the face.

All you have to do is look at one of the talk shows running rampant across our television screens to see every form of human misery caused by unsuccessful relationships. The horror stories from people who have been swindled out of their money/house/car/jewelry/lifestyle are myriad and never ending.

Granted: choosing a mate who is obviously an alcoholic or drug addict or murderer or any other of the many poor choices is a rotten idea. But how many people do you know who has someone of this description in her/his life?

After all if the person described is your parent or grandparent or child, you haven't exactly chosen this scenario.

So what are we talking about when we say, "Develop relationships that support your best self?"

We have to take this one word at a time.

"Develop" means that you have to start where you are and work toward the ideal. No one is foolish enough to believe that we are born into a world where perfect relationships are formed prior to our birth. We are born into an environment and we have to cope as best we can—when we begin at our most vulnerable stage of life!

No one has a perfect parent.

As an adult you have many aspects of your personality that are in response to this fact. You can spend the rest of your life blaming your caretaker or you can correct the situation through whatever means you have available or can learn about.

I have known people in the last years of their lives who were still angry at something a grandparent did when the person was five years old. How productive is this to anyone?

I have known of cases where a person literally destroyed his field of choices (engaging in criminal activity to the point he was incarcerated before he was 21) in order to "get even" with a parent he didn't think did a good enough job of rearing him.

NEWS BULLETIN: People do the best they can at the time.

That doesn't mean that what they do is right or smart or even kind. It means that using the feelings/knowledge/information they have at the time of the act, they choose what appears to be their best option. It doesn't mean that it is the best option. It means they do it and live to take the consequences.

The old adage of "walking in my moccasins" is a basic truth. We are all armchair quarterbacks in the game of life. We can sit back and criticize everyone from ourselves to our parents to our teachers to the President of the United States—and that's not wrong, because that's one of the ways in which we learn to make better decisions.

BUT we can't change the past.

What's done is done. What actions have already taken place are history. We can react to the consequences, but we can't change the past.

So if we find ourselves in a relationship that is harmful or damaging to our self concept,
The way out is to look within.
What is it in my makeup that caused me to make this choice? Do I have a need to "save Johnny from his drinking" or to "know that I am loved only if I entice someone else's husband away from her" or to "prove that I am more intelligent than my partner by beating him at his chosen profession" or what!
Here we are at the gateway to our self esteem.
If our self-esteem system is based on believing that we are going to be a more successful person if we have rescued Johnny from his excessive drinking (never mind that we are drinking right along with him!), then we are going to maintain a relationship that:

1. depends on Johnny's continued drinking—so we can rescue him, and
2. encouraging Johnny constantly to stop drinking, but giving him other messages that let him know we are going to continue to tolerate this pattern, never mind.

To digress for a moment, in my opinion, most programs that are touted as the answers for addictions of whatever kind fail in several ways:

1. They teach the person that s/he is always going to be weak and a victim of this illness.
2. They retain behavior but do not seek the root-level cause of the problem.
3. They focus on the addiction itself without getting into the heart of the addict.

Consequently, the person may stop drinking/using drugs/ overeating, whatever; but, the person may then accept some other addiction as a substitute.
I have known many "recovering alcoholics" who either drink "secretly" from then on, or become compulsive spenders or live in

squalor beyond belief. They are constantly reminding themselves that "I am an alcoholic" yet they choose as their closest friends other alcoholics.

My point is that the lowered self-esteem that caused the problem is still not addressed. To beat yourself for the rest of your life because you broke your back would be ludicrous, but to beat yourself because you chose to drink rather than to solve your problems is commonly accepted as proper behavior.

Depression is, in my opinion, the underlying cause of most addictions. If you find yourself drinking too much or smoking too much or using drugs to cope with everyday life, ask yourself why you are angry with yourself.

DEPRESSION IS ANGER TURNED INWARD.

If someone you love is depressed, try to help the person focus on what anger s/he is beating her/himself with.

Too many times people are carrying the burden of guilt for a problem over which they had little or no control; yet they have internalized the idea that it is wrong to be angry or it is unforgivable to be furious with a parent or other person for an injustice that person inflicted.

Releasing guilt is extremely difficult. We feel guilty that we were not in control of a situation to the point that we could have prevented it.

Any victim of rape can tell you that the worst result of the experience was her anger at herself for not preventing this event from happening to her. The anger that she feels toward the rapist is horrible, but it is inconsequential compared to the anger that she feels towards herself.

In order to deal with any behavior that is out of control, you have to determine why you want to engage in that behavior.

Many times lack of self-esteem is caused by knowing that you can have better circumstances in your life but you know you are not bringing the choices that bring them about.

If you are unhappy with your job, your marriage, your lack of love, your financial circumstances, whatever—you have to examine yourself, your attitudes, your beliefs in order to choose a better path. As a beginning in that direction, we are now going to list as many things as possible that we like about ourselves—right here, right now:

1.

2.

3.

4.

5.

6.

7.

8.

9.

10.

11.

12.

13.

14.

15.

Now we're going to list some aspects of us that we aren't pleased with:

1.

2.

3.

4.

5.

6.

7.

8.

9.

10.

11.

12.

13.

14.

15.

Do you need more quiet time in your life so that you can think about what you want to accomplish? If so, how are you going to get it?

List the changes you want to make in your relationships. And beside each, list what you are willing to do about yourself and your response to life in order to get what you want.

This list may become a list of the traits you want to have in your significant other, or it may be a list of the traits you appreciate but would like more of.

It's your list. You decide what your goals for your support system are.

For instance, are you willing to take your spouse out to dinner once a week (if that's what has been requested of you) as a swap for one night every two weeks at the bowling alley with a group of coworkers?

Are you willing to compliment your spouse every time s/he does something that pleases you rather than just assuming that person knows how you feel?

Are you willing to stop complaining about Johnny's drinking if he agrees to limit himself to one beer a night?

Here's your chance to make a commitment to a better life:

IN ORDER TO GET: I'M WILLING TO GIVE:

1.   1.

2.   2.

3.   3.

4.   4.

5.   5.

6.   6.

7.   7.

8.   8.

9.   9.

Now, what if the other person refuses to negotiate?
Then you have to get some serious decision making into play.
In any situation, you have three choices:

1. Accept things as they are.
2. Change whatever you see as the sources of your unhappiness or displeasure.
3. Leave.

Certain aspects of life should never be accepted. Willful infliction of pain—physical or psychological—should never be tolerated. If your significant other hits you or verbally abuses you and that person is unwilling to seek counseling or stop the abuse, it is up to you to leave. You can't begin to heal from these terrible wounds until they are no longer being inflicted.

Don't assume that because you are being verbally abused, you have no wounds. It can take years-as anyone in this room can attest—to heal from unkind and painful remarks.

I can give an example from my own childhood.

My great-grandmother was absolutely furious when my great-grandfather, her husband, died. She had built her life on the assumption that he would outlive her. She remained stuck in that anger, the angry stage of grief, for the rest of her life. It affected every thing she did, every way she acted, every word she spoke.

When I was about ten, I went through a stage of looking at my face in the mirror. Like most preteens, parts of my face were growing faster than others and I looked like a gangly colt.

One day my great-grandmother saw me looking in the mirror. With great malice, she pronounced, "You aren't pretty! Don't even bother looking at yourself in that mirror. You're not pretty at all!"

Reeling under the confirmation of my worst fears, I mumbled something like, "Oh, I was just seeing if I had any dirt on my face."

Inside, I was dying. I had been terrified that I was ugly and now here was the ultimate pronouncement of the fact. The matriarch of my childhood world had said it. It was true beyond a shadow of a doubt.

From that day forward, I knew that I was homely and reacted to life accordingly. It didn't matter if someone said I looked pretty. I knew that wasn't the case.

Not every child would have reacted to a remark like this as I did, of course. I had been reared to respect adults and to accept their words as gospel. It didn't even occur to me to say, "You're entitled to your opinion" or "At least I'm not crabby!" or worse.

As a child, you are vulnerable in a very special way. Some children avoid unpleasant scenes by staying in their rooms or by playing outside away from the adult world. Some resort to living totally in a world of fantasy: some even develop extra personalities or become autistic in extreme circumstances.

Whatever the situation you are confronting, you need to remember one thing:

YOU ARE RESPONSIBLE FOR THE BEHAVIOR OF ONLY
ONE PERSON.

YOU!!!!

When you truly accept that your spouse's behavior is his/her responsibility, you are freed from some extremely complicated and self-degrading feelings.

YOU DID NOT—DID NOT—DID NOT—MAKE ANY OTHER PERSON DO IT!

And, conversely,

NO ONE ELSE MADE YOU DO IT!!!!

One of the major problems in our society is that no one is responsible. Murderers did not nail another person's hands to the floor and steal their money after having raped the person because they are low, mean, murdering criminals. They have various syndromes or had lousy childhoods or whatever their defense attorney can dream up and convince the jury of without allowing the blame to fall on their client.

The fact remains: at some point in time, the person who committed the act made the decision to do it. The victim is dead.

Whatever life throws at each of us, it is our response to that fact that produces either positive or negative results.

Two people, through circumstances outside their control, lose all their money. One goes bankrupt and gives up. The other gets three jobs and recovers more than was lost originally. Same beginning, different response.

If you have angry feelings about what is going on in your life, you have to address these feelings, understand why you are angry and commit yourself to a positive way of releasing these angry feelings.

If you don't, you will become either physically ill or depressed or even suicidal. The physical illness may manifest itself through high blood pressure, ulcers, even a stroke or heart attack.

Anger is a legitimate feeling.

Holding anger inside is a time bomb. It has to come out one way or another.

A simple statement, "I feel angry when…." can begin to help. You must admit your anger; you must verbally acknowledge you anger; you must address the cause and then make some type of change that alleviates the situation.

I knew a woman who made her home with her husband, an only child, and his mother. The mother was extremely difficult. The woman would become justifiably angry with her mother-in-law. In order not to create more unpleasantness in her home, she would drive into the country where no one else was around and scream out her anger. She acknowledged that she was angry, she yelled out her rage, she got it out of her system for the time being, and she went back to the situation in control of herself.

If you have an acquaintance or loved one who is consumed by hatred, bless this person on his/her way. Life is too short to spend with hatred in the pathway of your becoming.

Release you anger—your hatred—the people who want to hold on to these feelings—to the universe. Let the universe deal with the problem.

Get on with your life.

The same scenario goes for jealousy. A jealous person looks at someone else and hates that person for having something s/he wants to have. What wasted energy!

If you want to be beautiful, it doesn't make you more beautiful to be jealous of a person you think is beautiful. Having cranky feelings about that person gives you wrinkles, not the other person. If you are crabby, you are less beautiful than you could be—and the other person hasn't lost a thing. If you spend the same amount of time and energy on washing your hair, putting on make-up or polishing you nails as you waste on feeling jealous of someone else, you have made a step towards your goal.

If you want to be a CEO of your company, add to your knowledge. Take classes at night, read, attend seminars. Don't sit around being an armchair jockey and hating your boss. Spend your time on constructive activities that will get you where you want to go.

Whatever your situation, you can:

1. Accept it.
2. Change it.
3. Leave.

If the people around you are constantly knocking you down, you're in the wrong place.

If you have a pattern in your life of choosing people around you who lower your self-esteem, examine your own attitudes about yourself and see if these people are mirroring your beliefs about yourself.

Are you acting clumsy because you think you're clumsy—then they are pointing out that you are clumsy—and the circle goes on!

What are you gaining from being clumsy?

Most likely, it's attention.

Acknowledge that there are better ways of getting attention than by being clumsy.

Reinforce the parts of your life for which you get positive attention. Concentrate on these methods of positive behavior and soon you won't be as clumsy as you once believed.

Choosing relationships that support your best self begins, as does everything else in life, with your attitudes about YOU.

If you love yourself enough to believe you deserve a loving significant other who will be supportive of you in the ways you need, you will attract a loving mate.

If you hold in your mind abusive attitudes about yourself, you will attract abuse. It's almost as if you had a sign on your back that reads, "Kick me."

If you've already attracted an abusive other, you can change your attitudes about yourself to the point that the other person will have to acknowledge that change and act accordingly, or the person will no longer be in your life.

You have the key inside yourself.

The word "repent" does not mean to beat yourself for what you have done wrong, the way most people have interpreted this word in our society. Repent comes from a Greek word that means "turn your mind."

If you "turn your mind" to loving thoughts and accept this love at the deepest level of your consciousness, you can change your life.

Norman Cousins wrote, "Nature has not been equally lavish with her endowments, but each man has his own potential in terms of achievement and service. The awareness of that potential is the discovery of purpose; the fulfillment of that potential is the discovery of strength."

EVENTUALLY THE GOOD YOU EXUDE COMES BACK TO YOU

Life can seem bitterly unfair at times. That's because it is very difficult to see that any good can arise from a bad situation.

In each person are characteristics that the person accepts and characteristics that the person denies. Psychiatrists tell us that we marry someone who has those characteristics that we deny in ourselves. We love the person initially because those traits seem wonderful and exciting and appealing. After we live with those traits a while, they are a pain in the posterior.

We look at life either from the light or from the shadow. We cannot see from both simultaneously.

When a traumatic event occurs in our own life, we see only the "bad" initially. If we are robbed, we feel the loss. We experience anger at the robber. We feel outraged at the injustice. We feel guilt that we did not do something to have prevented this loss. We feel remorse that we could not foresee the future.

If we have gained some degree of wisdom, we learn from the experience. We learn that we must not leave the car unlocked, or we must not park in a "bad neighborhood," or we must not leave items in plain view on the seat of the vehicle, or we must install an alarm system to deter thieves. We see how the escalation of this event could have resulted in personal injury or even loss of life and we are grateful that the problem was not worse.

When we become infatuated with another person, we see him/her as all wonderful, all beautiful, all desirable. As we continue the relationship, we see the person as having some good qualities and some less-than-desirable attributes.

If we continue to be close to the other person, we fall out of infatuation. We do not believe the other person to be all-knowing, all near perfection.

At this point, we begin to enter love. Love is a state of acceptance, acceptance of the other person just as s/he is, not as we wish her/him to be.

In a truly loving relationship, friendship is the common denominator with affection as the tie that binds. To know that you have truly found the significant other who can be your life partner, you must recognize that your support of this person's well-being must equal his/her support of your well-being.

Well-being occurs when you are in pursuit of your highest good. To demand that the other person subordinate all his/her desires to yours is not to love.

Granted, in any relationship, at some point one person has his/her way and the other waits. But the basic foundation for the relationship is that both people are in pursuit of their own personal success which is in harmony with the success of the other person.

When two people are in the infatuation stage of their relationship, they gaze deeply into the eyes of the other. It is as though each is searching for the answers to all his/her questions through the soul of the other—which basically is what each is doing.

When this stage has given way to a more balanced view, the couple can begin to pursue his/her own pathway again.

However, the emotional link gained at the initial stage serves as a framework for the continued success of each. It is important to recognize that the sharing of daily experiences becomes the glue of any relationship. It is important to share one's joys and triumphs, one's frustrations and disappointments, one's reaching of plateaus and sinking into the quagmire with one's significant other.

More relationships break up because people have lost daily contact than for any other reason.

Each of us grows and changes constantly. If you communicate one day that you can't stand black olives to your significant other and later you learn to enjoy black olives as much as any other food you've ever liked—and you don't communicate this—you may have dinner at a friend's house and rave over the black olives in the salad. Depending on the frame of mind of your significant other, s/he may be furious. S/he may think that the host is a potential lover for you because "when I gave you black olives, you had a temper tantrum and told me that you hated them!"

This is the type of message that gets extrapolated from "nothing" into a major trauma.

What is going on is that the significant other feels out of touch, abandoned, betrayed.

Emotions are one of the least controllable aspects of any relationship. This little scene over a type of food could easily have had its origins in a family meal when the significant other was a small child. The tape from the first event may play itself out in the adult without the adult having any conscious idea about its origin.

KEEP IN TOUCH WITH YOUR MATE

Many men will refuse to discuss "small talk." They consider only ideas about "important matters" to be worthy of their attention. A person who blocks out all day-to-day communication is doomed to a life of loneliness—and so is his mate unless she compensates in some other way.

A police officer was married to a reporter. The police officer was selfish and inconsiderate. He constantly ran up bills and made it very difficult for the reporter to make ends meet. She was always juggling money just to keep their finances in some state other than chaos.

Eventually, he left her for another woman. She went on with her life and one day found him back on her doorstep.

He said, "I came to ask your forgiveness."

"What do you mean?" she asked.

"I know now what I put you through and I'm terribly sorry for the way I mistreated you," he explained. "When I married the person I left you for, I found out that she had no sense of responsibility. I was always scratching and digging for enough money to pay the bills. She ran up monstrous bills everywhere and then she would quit her job and I would be scrambling to keep the electricity on and the landlord from evicting us.

"Everything I did to you, I had done to me ten times over," he admitted. "She's gone from my life now and it is such a relief. I want you to know that I can see myself as I was. I know now how hard I made your life. I'm truly, truly sorry. I want you to know that I understand that you will never take me back. I don't deserve it. But if there is ever anything I can do to help you, please know that I will. I have learned the hardest lesson I have ever had to swallow.

"I had to take back what I gave out."

Jesus was not trying to be a "nice guy" when he said, "Whatsoever you sow, thereof shall you reap."

He was trying to tell us that it's going to come back—good, bad, indifferent.

One of the basic laws of physics is "For every action there is an equal and opposite reaction."

That applies not only to physical matter but to the behavior of human beings as well.

I know that I can give you a hundred examples of someone who seemed to "get by" with things.

And I can give you a hundred where they didn't in the end.

When I was in high school a clique of boys ran the politics of our class. One of them, whom I'll call Ashton, was the leader of the pack. In the eyes of our principal, Ashton could do no wrong.

The Christmas of my sophomore year I belonged to a club for girls. We had a dance to which each of the members invited a date. One of my best friends, Rita, had a date with Ashton. I had a date with Ashton's sidekick, David, and my other girlfriend, Janet, had a date with Jonathon, third member of the clique.

We had asked these guys to the dance about six weeks in advance. Some time around Thanksgiving, Ashton began dating Mona, a member of another club. You guessed it. They were also having a Christmas dance and it just happened to fall on the same night as our dance.

We speculated as to whether or not Ashton would ask Rita to go to our dance with someone else so that he could take Mona to her dance—but he didn't.

The night of our dance I got a call from David. Ashton had had a death in his family and had to leave for Arkansas to go to the funeral. Would I mind if Rita went along with Jonathon and Janet and us on our double date? Of course, I said it would be fine and how sorry I was about Ashton's tragedy.

Again, you guessed it. Ashton took Mona to her dance. It was all over school by the time we got back from Christmas vacation.

I never went out with David again or had anything else to do with the guys in that "rat pack."

Years later, Ashton made the headlines in our hometown newspaper. He had left his wife and children, had run off to another country where he had frequently gone during his political career, and had run out of money. To support the new woman in his life, Ashton had decided to rob a bank. With the police hot on his trail, he made it back to his hotel room where he committed suicide.

Our high school principal was quoted as being absolutely astounded. I wasn't. Ashton had proved his character to me many years before.

If you live long enough, you see people who were in power and abused workers in their department then become abused by their bosses.

One manager systematically documented every minor error that one of his employees made until he was able to fire the person. In the meantime, the manager's boss was systematically documenting every mistake he made—and within a few weeks, the manager himself was fired!

The characteristics we dislike the most in other people are the characteristics of our own personalities that we shun the most. If you find yourself being super critical of someone else, stop and look at your own behavior. Be prepared to clean up your own workshop!

So, how are some ways that the good you exude comes back to you?

Smiles. It's amazing how smiling at someone becomes contagious. Try it. Some people won't smile back, of course, because they have not formed a habit of having a pleasant look on their faces. But most people will. You never know what a smile can do for someone else. It might just make all the difference in the world.

At the very least, a smile can make the other person wonder what you're up to!

Here's another way your good comes back to you—knowledge. When you share what you know with someone else, that knowledge enhances the other person's life. Perhaps that person then shares the newfound experience with someone else. Usually you have forgotten about it, but the other person may not have.

One day I ran into a former neighbor, someone I hadn't seen in several years.

He said something that took me totally by surprise. He said, "I want to thank you for saving my marriage. You talked to my wife one day and convinced her to be her own person. It totally changed our lives around and we've been on the right road ever since."

Needless to say, his words warmed my heart.

Years ago I taught school in Florida in a very small town. My second year as the first full-time music teacher for the elementary school I directed and sang in "Amahl and the Night Visitors." It was the first opera—and maybe its last, for all I know—for that community.

It was one of the magical times when the right people were in the right place to be able to pull this feat off. We had a high school choral teacher who was a marvelous pianist; he played the extremely difficult accompaniment to perfection. We had another teacher who had just finished college and had a gorgeous tenor voice. He also had acting experience and was able to play Amahl very convincingly.

Three events arose from that opera that will always be with me.

One was a very small boy who was in kindergarten that year. He was the absolute terror of the class. His teacher made him sit right next to her during the opera for fear he would "act up."

In the opera there are the three wise men and their page. A very massive football player named Tiny played the role of Page. During the opera the mother (the role I sang) tries to steal the gold that the wise men are taking to the Christ Child; she is anguished because Amahl has no food due to her poverty. Just as she crawls across the floor and touches the gold, the Page wakes up and grabs her, yelling, "Thief!"

When this happened on stage, the little boy from the kindergarten class grabbed his teacher and begged, "Save her! Save her!"

When the teacher told me about this after the performance, I knew that all our long hours of hard work had been worthwhile.

The second thing that I remembered was a young girl who was about twelve. She stopped me on the sidewalk about a week after the opera and said, "In all my life I have never seen anything like this. I shall never forget it as long as I live."

The third was a thank you letter I received. It was from the mother of three of our children who attended the school. The woman had muscular dystrophy and was rearing these children alone after their father, upon finding out that his wife had this terrible disease, left her, saying, "I'm too young to spend my life with a cripple."

Of all the parents in the school, this woman wrote to thank me for bringing this experience to her children.

The good comes back to you. Believe me. Sometimes more than you have ever dreamed of.

LET GO OF THE PAST, LIVE IN THE PRESENT AND KNOW THAT YOUR INNER RESOURCES ARE SUFFICIENT NO MATTER WHAT THE FUTURE BRINGS

What a mouthful!

Let's take it a little at the time:

Let go of the past.

What does that mean? Don't I mean "Learn from the past?"

Nope. I mean **LET GO!**

So how does one go about letting go of the past!

First, you have to confront whatever has gone on in your life that you are still dragging around with you. Nobody knows everything that you are carrying like an anchor in your heart but you.

Are you still angry at a kid in third grade who tripped you in front of a girl you were trying to impress and made you feel like a fool?

Are you still fuming over the way your mother always told you you were clumsy and couldn't walk and chew gum simultaneously?

Have you hidden animosities towards the college professor who gave you a "C" on your final when you needed a "B" to keep from having to take another course in astronomy?

I don't know what you are making yourself miserable with, but you do.

Maybe you are mad at yourself more than anyone else? Do you still cringe when you think of the time you made a cutting remark about someone only to look around and see the person right behind you?

Are you furious over the fact that you weren't able to do anything to prevent being raped?

Do you think you will never get over the humiliation of having your marriage fail?

We all carry around in our souls angry, bitter, hurtful feelings from incidents in our past. But has anyone of these leftover emotions ever helped us, or anyone else for that matter? Of course not.

Yet we continue to beat ourselves internally for what we should have done, or what we could have done.

And we suffer needlessly.

The past is over.

Yes, hopefully we have learned from the past so that we don't have to make the same mistake again. But if we haven't learned from the past and the same issue confronts us again, we'll make the same mistake or another one until we get it right. That's called learn by doing and we all have this aspect of life to encounter on a daily basis.

So what about letting go of the past?

That's the way to keep healthy, both mentally and physically. If we continue to churn and churn these terrible things from the past in our minds, we shall either get a physical disease like ulcers or high blood pressure or cancer, or a mental disease like depression or neurosis or even psychosis!

How does one let go of the past?

It's the easiest thing and the hardest thing you'll ever do, but it's also one of the most worthwhile experiences you can ever have.

It's easy because it frees you of the terrible burden of carrying a dead carcass in your heart. That's what past emotions, past hatreds, past angers are—dead carcasses. The past is dead. There is not one blessed thing you can ever do to change it. You can wish it were different. You can hallucinate that it was different. But you can't go back and undo it.

The past is over and done with, both now and forever more. So dump it! That's right. Dump it out of your heart.

One simple way to get rid of the past is to write it down and destroy it.

Some people have to write an entire book to dump it; others have to write only a word and burn the piece of paper; others have to see themselves filling a garbage bag—the size of their choice—and dumping it over the edge of a cliff.

What you have to do to get rid of the past is make a definite and conscious effort to obliterate the unpleasant happenings however it works for you.

You can see yourself shoving all the past hurts and angers and disappointments into a seven-story office building, locking the door and then blowing the entire thing up with dynamite.

You can imagine you have weighted down all the past you want to get rid of in a giant garbage bag and have flung it into the hottest volcano on earth.

Whatever works for you, do it. Do it now. Don't carry these misery-provoking feelings into one more second of the present. Dump it, blow it up, burn it up, fling it into the farthest reaches of the universe, zap it with a laser gun!

And be free.

That's what letting go of the past is all about—allowing yourself to be free.

Again, the Greek word from which our word "repent" comes means "turn your mind."

That's what letting go of the past allows you to do—turn your mind from life-wasting anguish that makes you miserable and keeps you from living in the present and enjoying the future. It's like focusing on the smelliest garbage pit one minute and turning your head to smell the most gorgeous flower on earth the next.

It's your choice.

Let go. You can't go back and change anything so just let go of it. Channel your energies into the present. Give yourself wholeheartedly into being now and making a difference in the world. Just by becoming your best self, rather than flailing yourself for your past mistakes, you are creating a better world for everyone else as well.

A very small book called *Love Is Letting Go of Fear* by Dr. Gerald Jampolski teaches a profound truth. Dr. Jampolski worked with children who were dying of cancer. Many times they were in acute pain. He learned that by focusing their mind on love instead of fearing the pain, they could actually override the pain to the extent that they no longer experienced it.

If you don't believe this, try to think of a time when you were sick and lying on the couch watching television. A very funny sequence comes on. You become so involved in watching it and laughing at it that you literally leave your illness, even if it's only for a few seconds.

The principle is the same as is used in the Lamaze method of childbirth. A woman learns to concentrate her attention so completely on one spot that she does not feel the terrible pains of childbirth.

The medical community is just beginning to understand endorphins, chemicals in the brain that are released to give a feeling of well-being. They truly promote healing of the physical body. They are released by laughter and happiness.

If you find yourself ill in some way, try creating as much laughter in your life as possible. Years ago Norman Cousins, the man who wrote a biography of Albert Schweitzer, had a severe heart attack. He was told he had a very short time to live. He locked himself in a hotel room with scores of funny movies and became much healthier. He lived, in fact, much longer than he was told he ever could.

He wrote about his experiences, but many people thought he was crazy.

Now scientific evidence is confirming what Norman Cousins found out for himself. Attitude has everything to do with your mental and physical health.

An old man once said to me, "Health, wealth and happiness: notice the order they are in. I have more money than most of the people on earth will ever have, but it does me no good whatsoever unless I have my health."

Be good to yourself. Eat right, sleep enough, cling to healthy attitudes, allow yourself to accept from this world whatever you need.

Surround yourself if at all possible with people who have positive, healthy attitudes. Don't let people drag you down. Don't drag other people down. Keep smiling—and the world will smile back at you. And if they don't, keep smiling anyway because you know you have the secret of being happy inside you. You are the voice of reason when you turn loose of the past. You have conquered your fears in a very special way.

Fear is a bucket that churns your negative feelings into monsters and bogey men that terrify you for no reason.

My father says, "Most of the things you worry about never happen. The few that do are ones you can't do anything to stop anyway, so what's the point of worrying. It never helps."

Worrying is jumping up and down in fear and whipping your fears into reality.

Remember: thoughts held in mind produce after their kind.

If you are constantly worrying that something terrible is about to happen, you may wake up and find it happening because you have set the stage for it.

Just like Grumpy said in *Snow White and the Seven Dwarfs*, "I've been telling you boys for 500 years that something terrible was about to happen."

Fear releases harmful chemicals into your bloodstream. Your body has to fight them off. If your resistance is down, your body is overwhelmed and you get sick.

Think about the times you get a cold. Aren't you overtired? Aren't you upset about something that is going on in your life? Are you clearing something away that you have either outgrown or didn't want in the first place?

Your body is throwing off something. You collapse in bed if you are smart and let it come up and out. If you keep on dragging around, it will take longer to get well and you may get something else as well. Listen to your body. Keep your spirits high. Be well and happy. Your life will be much more productive.

If you become ill, ask yourself, "How is this illness serving me?" Most of the time, your illness is either getting you attention from someone from whom you were reluctant to ask for it, or it is helping you avoid something you don't want to do. Be honest with yourself.

It's okay to be sick sometimes. Everybody is. It would be ideal if we all felt comfortable enough with the people we love to say, "I feel like I would like to be pampered today. It would be wonderful to have breakfast in bed, read for a while and take an extra nap. Would you mind taking care of me today, and another day I'll do the same for you?" But we don't.

So sometimes we get sick. We're really sick too. We run a fever and we cough and we throw up and other wretched things happen. We're justified to stay home and stay in bed.

It's okay.

But it's much better to feel well.

Letting go of the past can produce not only a sense of well-being but of euphoria. Hating always hurts the person who hates; being angry churns up the emotional well-being of the one who is angry; fear grips the soul of the person who is fearful.

Let go. You won't be sorry. You'll be free—at last! And it's okay if you have to let go again. Let go until it's all gone forever.

It took me 25 years to let go of being violated but I finally got rid of it. You can too.

Once you have let go, you can live in the present. What am I talking about—you already live in the present, you say!

Great, if you do. I sometimes find that I have pre-rehearsed tapes that come rolling out of my mouth that I've learned when I was a child or in another situation and I wasn't even aware that they were there.

I'll bet you have a few tapes yourself.

If your father used to get inebriated when he had a problem weighing on his mind, you might utilize this tape on occasion without ever realizing its origin.

If your mother got hysterical when someone walked across the rug with muddy feet, you might too. See what I mean? We all have learned responses to certain situations. We can relearn the way we would like to respond to the point that it is automatic eventually, but it takes effort.

When you begin to live in the present, you begin to flow with whatever is happening. We all know people who have certain routines and rituals they follow.

For instance, some people have to drink two cups of coffee with cream and sugar every morning before they can speak to anyone else. Other people need to have a bowl of cereal just before they retire in order to get a good night's sleep.

If you live in the present, you may be in a habit of drinking coffee immediately after you wake up, but chances are, if someone discovers a few deer walking across your lawn and that person wakes you to show you their beauty, you can forego a cup of coffee until after you've tried to capture them on film.

You can live in the present and make daily "to do" lists, but if something interrupts your day and you can't finish what you planned, you can cope with putting some things off until another day.

You learn to know that whatever lesson life has for you in that moment, you can be open and receptive to it. That doesn't mean you are always running willy nilly; it just means you can accept change.

Change is inevitable. In life, either you grow and change or you die. There are no other alternatives.

Consider your skin. The type of skin you had when you were a baby is not the same type of skin you have as an 80-year-old. No one in their right mind expects to see baby-like skin on an older person, but we expect people to act relatively the same all their lives.

When our grandmother begins to be more frank with her opinion, we are flabbergasted. "She must be getting senile!" we think to ourselves. "She never used to say things like that."

But the truth may be that Grandmother doesn't have time for false appearances and sham in her life. She wants to call a rose a rose and she doesn't pull any punches to do that. In general, it's true. The older you get, the less of society's pretense you are able to tolerate. Hopefully, age and wisdom go hand in hand.

You begin to see that racing to the destination is not what life is about. The journey is indeed more important than the destination.

Watch drivers on the road. Some people are passing everything on the road because they think that those very few seconds they are gaining are more important than safety. Others have a steel grip on the steering wheel as they focus on the road ahead. And occasionally, you see someone really enjoying the ride. They are looking at the beautiful trees and flowers, they see the glint of sunlight on the roof of an old barn, they enjoy the sunset.

Which one are you?

When you live in the present, you enjoy each day for the beauty it holds.

You are grateful for whatever happiness you can experience—the excitement of getting closer to a goal, the warmth of the smile of a friend, the accomplishment of one more book you have read.

And as you accomplish your goals—the small ones at first, and the larger ones at last—you begin to acquire the knowledge that you are capable of meeting whatever life has to throw at you. You begin to welcome challenge, to acknowledge new heights to climb, to create objectives you could never have dreamed of before.

Your inner voice begins to praise you more often. You experience a feeling of contentment and of well-being that holds you even through the worst of times.

You recognize that when something appears to fail, it is actually pointing you in the direction of success.

You love yourself, you love life, you are spiritually whole.